About Frankie Armstrong

Frankie Armstrong was born in Cumbria and grew up within an extraordinarily warm and loving family. She was an active youngster, who acted, swam, sang with a skiffle band and, briefly, dated Cliff Richard.

She trained as a social worker and has worked extensively with drug addicts, while simultaneously developing her singing career. Her blindness, which began while she was in her teens, has led her to particularly develop folk singing and her voice therapy workshops, for which she is now universally known.

Frankie Armstrong is co-author, with Kathy Henderson and Sandra Kerr, of *My Song is My Own*, and she contributed to *Glancing Fires: An Investigation into Women's Creativity* (The Women's Press, 1987).

About Jenny Pearson

Jenny Pearson, a former journalist on *The Times*, has worked with the authors of several books, including Diana Rigg on *No Stone Unturned* and the late Sir Andrzej Panufik on *Composing Myself*. She is a drama and movement therapist, and a storyteller.

Frankie Armstrong with Jenny Pearson

As Far as the Eye Can Sing

First published by The Women's Press Ltd 1992
A member of the Namara Group
34 Great Sutton Street, London EC1V 0DX

British Library Cataloguing in Publication Data
Armstrong, Frankie
As Far as the Eye Can Sing
I. Title   II. Pearson, Jenny
782.42164092

ISBN 0 7043 4294 4

Typeset by Contour Typesetters, Southall, London
Printed and bound in Great Britain by
BPCC Hazells Ltd
Member of BPCC Ltd

*To the late Jim Armstrong,
my father, whose idea this book
originally was, and my
mother Dorothy, my oldest and
dearest friend.*

ACKNOWLEDGEMENTS

I would like to thank Sally O'Connor, Brian Pearson and Kathy Henderson for their invaluable help in reading and making suggestions in the early stages of writing this book; and Darien Pritchard for reading and helping with the penultimate draft and for his patience, generosity and for the numerous meals he fed me whilst I was glued to my computer.

To Moya Simpson for the title of the book.

To Jenny Pearson, without whom I would neve. have embarked on the project let alone finish it, who at every stage acted as my eyes and whose watchfulness has kept the threads of my story from unravelling.

To Kathy Gale for her inspired and patient editing.

Thanks to all those friends and colleagues, some of whom appear in the book and some of whom, for reasons of space, no longer appear by name, who have unstintingly given me of their love, support and inspiration throughout our friendships.

Lastly, to PC Plod, my talking computer, who gave me the independence and facility to put print to paper.

Prologue

4 June 1990, Moorfields Hospital

This is an auspicious day on which to begin a book. The admission procedures are over. My temperature, blood pressure and weight have all been pronounced normal, my heart sound. The inevitable urine samples have been given. Now there is no more to be done but wait until tomorrow.

Tomorrow I shall descend to the operating theatre for a cataract extraction – a straightforward enough procedure in itself, but a lifetime of complications (chiefly glaucoma and uveitis) means that fear tempers the hope. It may be that I shall regain some of my sight, now almost entirely gone, but there is a risk that I may lose what little sight I have. Or the operation may have no noticeable effect.

Sitting on my bed, I have enough sight to recognize where the windows are and to see the shadows of the nurses when, from time to time, they pass in front of the light. But I can't see the table-tray spanning the end of my bed or the people who share this hospital ward with me.

Whatever the outcome of the operation, there will be some change from my present situation – a major crossroads. And yet my overriding mood is one of calm and a sense of the extraordinary blessings that I am heir to. Much of my feeling of being blessed I owe to my parents, Dorothy and Jim Armstrong, who never wavered in their love and encouragement. I have come to realize that those of us who can truly say this of our parents are few. The time leading up to today's hospital admission has also made me profoundly aware of the number of friends, kindred spirits and soul mates whose love and support I have never valued more than I do now.

This is an interesting time, given the enforced period of idleness, to reflect on the path that has brought me thus far.

Early Years

Chapter 1

I was born in Workington, Cumbria. Good fortune was with me from the start – my earliest years were spent in the Lake District, one of the most beautiful, unspoilt areas in the British Isles. The stories surrounding my birth suggest that I was reluctant to leave the womb. An extended breech birth required two doctors and forceps to persuade me out into the chilly January evening. I was Dorothy Armstrong's firstborn and they eventually decided to gas her gently through the last part of the ordeal. As she came round, she heard the doctors declaring me 'perfect'. They were most likely expressing relief that the forceps delivery had left no mark on me, but Mum chose to interpret their statement in absolute terms.

I think the tale of my arrival in the world says something about my willingness to come out and play, provided the reception committee is large enough and sufficient notice is taken of the song and dance I make. I have grown to realize that the sense I carry of being at the centre of my own world is quite rare in women. The almost undivided attention of a self-sufficient, contented and ever curious mother for the first 18 months of life must have fostered this quality in me.

The advent of my brother Tony caused a slight hiccup in my feeling of universal wellbeing. I remember cutting off his lovely blond curls (which never grew back) and pushing him down the stairs, and once he retaliated by laying a red hot poker on my leg. But eventually we settled down and learnt to accept and be grateful for our differences.

When I was three we moved to the tiny village of Brigham in the northeast of the Lakes. I was hardly aware of the war until the village parade on VE Day, though I do remember clenching my eyes and teeth and stuffing my fingers in my ears when planes swooped low over the village. I also have a clear memory of my immensely tall and good-looking father in his Home Guard uniform, and of a certain evening when the blackout curtains were drawn across the kitchen window and both my parents watched me in my Viyella nightie, embroidered with rabbits, as I danced on the deal kitchen table and sang them a song:

> Lula, lula, lula, lula, bye bye,
> Do you want the stars to play with?
> The moon to run away with?
> You can if you don't cry.
> So lula, lula, lula, lula, bye bye,
> In Mummy's arms lie sleeping
> And soon you'll be dreaming, so
> Sing lula, lula, lula, lula bye.

My best friends, Brenda and Sally, lived at our end of the village and I recall us playing with our Ragetty Ann dolls and spinning old bicycle wheels happily up and down Brigham's single, traffic-free street. Brenda and Sally were older than me and hence, one dismal day, disappeared to a mysterious place called school. It was explained to me that they could go to school because they were five and I couldn't because I was four. I could see no sense in this: I could walk, talk and think for myself and argued that there was no reason why I shouldn't go to school too. I pestered Mum so insistently that she took my request seriously and put my case to the headmaster. To his great credit he listened to her argument and, after 'interviewing' me, agreed to let me join the class of five-year-olds.

So, to my huge delight, I was able to go with Brenda and Sally on the morning walk to school, half a mile along a country road. I have just one clear memory of it, etched like a Christmas card, everything white with blanketing snow except for the grey stone walls and the dark curve looming over our heads as we approached the cuckoo bridge. I wore Dutch clogs, as we nearly always did, and from time to time I found myself slithering on the snow. But I was so proud to be going to school with the big girls.

At the end of the war the aircraft plant in Workington, where my father was employed, was closed and Dad went down south to look for work, leaving us in our village. He found a job and digs at Brimsdown, near Enfield, Middlesex, and after six months he found accommodation where we could join him, sharing a house with a doctor and his wife.

From there, when I was six, we moved to the outskirts of a little market town, Hoddesdon, where my parents bought their first house, situated in a leafy, unmade road. This meant that much of my childhood was spent adventuring in the adjoining fields, blackberrying, climbing trees, and trespassing on private estates. The woods, fields, brooks, farms, animals and birds were the ever-present backdrop against which life was acted out.

Family pets were an almost constant presence. There was Whisky, a part Cairn terrier, Muffin the tabby, a crazy, aristocratic Siamese called Yeti, mice, guinea pigs, rabbits and budgerigars.

Whisky was with us for five or six years until his propensity for biting postmen's legs meant, sadly, that he had to be 'put to sleep'. We missed him terribly, feeling so angry and helpless when his otherwise gentle nature was undermined by the appearance of men in uniform, leading to his untimely end. I was intrigued and curious about this thing called 'death'. Apparently, when I was about three, a child died in Brigham and the whole village community turned out for his funeral. Mum tells me that she sat up with me far into the night, dealing with my questions and distress.

My constant interest and passion throughout my childhood and early teens was for drawing, painting and making puppets. I must have been three when, on a thinnish scrap of paper, I painted an orange face. From that moment on, pen or paintbrush was never long out of my hand. Dad used to bring home discarded accounting paper from work for me to draw and paint on the blank side. I would create scenes with ballet dancers, film stars, historical events, characters from books and, inevitably, horses. Just occasionally I would paint a landscape or a still life, but these were rare. It was expressions on faces, the line and flow of human figures and the movement of animals that excited me. Sometimes I traced things out of encyclopaedias or Mum's art books or my film books, but most often my pictures were conjured up out of my imagination.

I also read a lot at this time and developed a passion for the cinema, which went on for some years. I was a great fan of Rin Tin Tin and Tarzan, and later of the great Hollywood musicals.

At the age of six I was given my first voice lessons, by my drama and elocution teacher at school. Mum was already reciting Keats, Shelley and Matthew Arnold to me, so the most important influence came from home, but the lessons must have reinforced my love of words and what the human voice can create with them. At the same time my strong Cumbrian accent was outlawed and I was indoctrinated with 'correct' pronunciation through the 'How now brown cow' routine – an imposition that still makes me angry when I think about it.

My first theatrical break was playing the lead in the school performance of *The Pied Piper of Hamelin*. It was to be a seminal performance as it gave me my first notice in a newspaper. The *Hoddesdon Journal* may not be the most prestigious place for one's first review, but on reading it now I still feel affection for the writer and consider him a person of discernment and perception!

> Leading the way was the Pied Piper, played by Frances Armstrong, who was excellent as the merry Piper . . . for besides leading the children of the fairytale village away into the land of make-believe, her convincing performance also 'carried away' the large audience . . .

Throughout my schooling (I prefer not to call it education, since most of that was acquired after I left school) I loved

English and drama. I played a number of parts in school plays, which remain clear and bright in my memory. But by the age of 13 or 14 my imaginative world was already beginning to dim. Today I am slowly journeying back to this bright world, especially through story, song, myth and drama.

I enjoyed my first year at grammar school and did quite well academically, receiving one of the three first-year prizes, but academic decline had already started. It seemed that to stay in the prize-winning league I would have to spend a fair amount of otherwise free time studying and doing homework. To my mind, the trade-off wasn't worth it. Quite simply, I was more interested in horses, swimming and friends. I recall my year mistress saying disapprovingly, 'Frances, you seem to be the kind of pupil who achieves maximum results for the minimum of effort!' I felt this to be an achievement!

My freedom to come and go on my own was established early on: Dad insisted that if I was to grow up responsible, I had to be free to exercise responsibility. At first Mum resented this: she was often sleepless with worry, pacing to the front window to look for my bike light coming home. But with hindsight we both thank him: the independence and trust that have taken me through my life were born of that early experience.

I joined the swimming club and quickly made a circle of friends who met and trained there evening after evening. There was a period when I would also get up an hour and a half earlier than usual to cycle a mile and a half to the pool, swim madly up and down for half an hour and then cycle home for breakfast, before catching the bus to school. Soon the swimming pool became more important than school. I had thought about going to university and studying art or art history, for I still loved drawing, but gradually that idea faded. The art teacher's repeated demands that I produce realism and accuracy felt like a stranglehold.

And then I began to sing in groups and my interest in everything else started to wane. At last, one sunny afternoon in July 1957, I stood at the 310 bus stop for the last time and ceremoniously stuffed my school hat into my satchel.

'I do not and will not regret this day!' I thought. 'School days best days of your life? Pooh!' And I was right.

Chapter 2

I found my way into singing by doing it for enjoyment. As a child I loved listening to classical ballet music. This developed into a more general love of classical music, which remained with me through all the changing interests and discoveries that followed. But the piano lesson routine never really caught on. I did learn for a while, beginning when I was 11, and I wasn't bad at it, but neither was I particularly gifted or diligent. I don't remember taking any formal exams and what I learnt about musical theory would have fitted on a postage stamp. By the time I could manage Bach's *Sonata in C* and Beethoven's *Für Elise* I was riding and swimming and increasingly reluctant to sit down and 'do my scales'. One day my kind but not very inspiring teacher said there was no point in going on, since I wasn't prepared to put in the practice. My parents agreed and that was the end of the matter.

Then I had a short run of singing lessons, but that didn't last long either. I was much better in lively, informal situations. I would sing without inhibition on coach rides, at parties, and when the family gathered round the piano to sing songs out of *The Complete Home Entertainer*. I was in the school choir until I was thrown out for irregular attendance at choir practice. But by this time I was beginning to experiment out of school with less conventional ways of combining voices in song.

I went into glasses at the age of five, having been diagnosed as simply short-sighted. In my early teens I sometimes noticed my sight becoming cloudy or rainbow haloes forming around bright lights, which lasted for a matter of hours. As I was swimming at lot at this time, I put the effects down to the chlorine.

But during my 'mock' O Level exams, I found myself writing off the page on to the blotting paper. My ophthalmologist had been strengthening my glasses year by year, so that by the time I was 16 they were quite thick. I was worried that I might have serious difficulties when I came to take the proper exams, so I told Mum and Dad that I was going to see our GP and ask him for a referral to Moorfields Eye Hospital in London. But we miscalculated the power of medical paternalism and protectionism.

This GP had referred me to the County Ophthalmologist when I was five, and I suppose my request for a second opinion was taken as something of a slight. So instead of sending me to Moorfields he referred me to the County Hospital again, where I was taken in for a range of tests to see if they could find anything organically wrong. I spent a few dismal days in a general surgical ward, surrounded by dreary older women comparing notes on operations while I was given a going over to eliminate diabetes and who knows what else. I was discharged with a clean bill of health and told 'It's just your age. You'll get over it.'

Yet another change of glasses brought about a temporary improvement, enabling me to get through my exams, but the specialist advised me to leave school after taking O Levels. I was only too happy to oblige, and the following month I went to work at Liberty's, studying their designs with the idea of becoming a buyer and, perhaps, eventually designing fabrics myself.

And then, in October–November 1957, I took a month off to 'develop my character' at an Outward Bound School in Wales.

We were some twenty girls and young women staying in a sports and recreation centre in Snowdonia. We had a certain number of lectures on the local flora and fauna, map reading, orientation and regional history, but most of our time was spent out of doors on the mountains. We learnt rock-climbing and scrambling, how to handle a canoe and how to find our way back to the Centre, having been dropped off in the early morning darkness in groups of three at an unknown location 20 miles away.

I remember being rather homesick during the first week,

but then I got caught up in making new friends and feeling the stirrings of an addiction to mountains. I found myself excited and challenged by the experience. Rock climbing pushed me to my extremes, both physically and emotionally.

But it was on the climbs that I began to notice an alarming change in my vision. Before, I had experienced brief episodes of blurring, but now my sight was misty for days at a time.

One day when we were walking up the slopes of Moel Siabod, picking our way on slippery rocks above a fast-flowing stream, I realized I was losing my ability to judge the distance and angle of the rocks. It was very frightening. I confided this to Priscilla and Sally, the two special friends I had made, but felt unwilling to say anything to the adult tutors, as I feared it would seem like an excuse for special treatment. I remember new glasses arriving in the post and my intense disappointment that these only marginally improved my sight. It was at this point that I began to wonder whether there was something more seriously wrong than doctors and the eye specialist had told me.

I was faced with a dilemma: whether to give in and admit defeat or struggle on somehow. I felt I had had little understanding either from teachers or the medical profession, so it wasn't surprising that my response was a grim determination not to let the difficulties I was experiencing show, except to my two new-found confidantes. The rivers, the mountains, the lakes, the wild and often bleak autumnal landscape, became a solace in the face of this lonely fear, though I was later to discover that the exertions this landscape demanded of me helped to cause the irreversible loss of sight that took place over that month. However, I do not regret the experience, both because of the knowledge and love of mountains it gave me and because it accelerated the day when at last I was sent to Moorfields, where for the first time I was given a correct diagnosis and the treatment I needed.

On the last day of our stay we were given personal assessments. My report from the Director of the Outward Bound School said I was 'perhaps a little self-centred and not very forthcoming in helping others.' This may well have been true, though I think I can plead extenuating circumstances!

I arranged to see my eye specialist again when I returned from Wales and this time he made an appointment for me to be seen at Moorfields. We discovered that I must have had my major eye conditions from a very early age.

Strangely enough, this consultation was not the first visit I had made to Moorfields. Only days before that appointment, a group I was singing with had been invited to be part of the Nurses' Christmas Party (one of the group was going out with a Moorfields nurse at the time.) So on that December evening, I emerged for the first time from Old Street Station into the City Road to enter the imposing portals of this world-renowned eye hospital – not as a patient, but as a singer! This was only the first time that the threads of my sight and my singing came, quite bizarrely, together.

Chapter 3

I first sang publicly to strangers at an inter-church youth groups' social evening. My band consisted of my brother, another lad, Sue Ruskin and me, singing Elvis Presley and Little Richard numbers. Then I met a young man called Harry Webb, who played the guitar and sang. I found him very appealing and we dated for a while. My clearest recollection of our brief romance was of Harry bicycling through a winter storm, wearing his blue mac and stripy pompom hat, to come and visit me. We sat on the red upright sofa holding hands and listening to Pat Boone singing 'Chains of Love'. He was a genuinely sweet, gentle young man. He sent me a Christmas card which, had I kept it, could have been auctioned for a considerable sum a few years later, since Harry Webb was to become Cliff Richard. The last time I saw him 'live' was on a cycle pilgrimage to St Albans Abbey one Easter. He had a DA hairdo and was wearing pink fluorescent socks.

At another youth club social, in the spring of 1957, I heard my first skiffle group. It was the height of the trad jazz revival. I was drawn powerfully to the raw energy and immediacy of skiffle, and to the straightforward manner in which the songs were presented. I became a fanatical jiver at the weekly trad jazz club and there Mac Jones, leader of the Stort Valley Skiffle Group, asked me to dance. To my immense delight, he casually asked if I knew a 'girl singer' who might be interested in joining his band. There was only one answer: 'Yes – me!' And that was how it all began.

A few days later, Mac came to our house for a first rehearsal. I remember standing in the sun-filled room, full of anticipation and nervous excitement. Would I be good enough? Would he accept me into the group? I had learnt 'Freight Train', and Mac was accompanying me on his guitar. To my great relief, he liked what he heard.

A few weeks later, there I was, standing in the French Horn pub, surrounded by my four accompanists with that buzz of adrenalin that every performer needs to step out in front of an audience and give of her best. 'Freight Train', 'Trouble in Mind' and 'House of the Rising Sun' were the first songs I sang with the Stort Valley Skiffle Group.

There was no question about it – skiffle changed my life. I met artists, radicals and serious musicians and learnt to communicate feelings and ideas through song. I found it easy to identify with the creators of the songs we sang. Initially, they were the songs of the black and poor white peoples of the United States. Later they were the songs of the peasantry: land workers of the British Isles and Eire. The songs spoke of the happenings of everyday life – loving, feuding, working, suffering, dreaming and hoping. When I first sang them I knew little or nothing of their history or background, but something inside me was stirred by these stories, by the cries for freedom and affection.

None of us in the Skiffle Group were political in the party sense. In many ways, it was the singing of the songs that opened our small-town eyes to universal issues such as Civil Rights, the appalling conditions in mines and factories, the brutality and dangers of life at sea over the past centuries and women's outrage and sorrow as their husbands and sons were sent to war. Remembered at random, here are a few samples taken from songs we sang at this time.

I'm happy for to see you home,
Harroo, harroo,
I'm happy for to see you home,
Harroo, harroo.
I'm happy for to see you home
All from the island of Ceylon
So low in the flesh, so high in the bone,
Johnny, I hardly knew you.

Is it nothing to you if we haven't the right
To cast our vote for our skin's not white?
Kept down like slaves and tell me for why,
Is it nothing to you who pass by?

Do you care for us if we're lonely and old?
Or children left orphans when the death knell has tolled?
When fighting or fearing has wrecked all our lives,
Is it nothing to you who pass by?

Oh, what will you give me? say the sad bells of Rhymney.
Is there hope for the future? cry the brown bells of
Merthyr.
Who made the mine owner? say the black bells of
Rhondda.
And who robbed the miner? cry the grim bells of Blaina.

Many of the songs, however, were lighthearted, even
nonsensical, often with refrains and choruses for the audience
to join in. And, as they have been since time immemorial,
many of the songs were about love, often lost love,
frequently leading to tragedy for the women involved.

Oh love is tender, love is bonny,
A little while when first 'tis new,
But as love grows old it waxes cold
And fades away like morning dew.
I wish, I wish my babe was born
And smiling on his Daddy's knee,
And me poor girl was dead and gone
With green grass growing over me.

I still find very few love songs in other musical genres that
have the directness and truth that I hear in the traditional
love songs, for all their outdated idiom. And it is those two

qualities, 'directness' and 'truth', which explain why the best of traditional songs and stories speak to me with freshness and depth after all these years. They were created from inner need to give form and shape to human experience and to voice it. Not all folk songs are great art, but for me folk song at its best encompasses a wider range of emotion, situation and experience than is found in other song forms.

Such songs served as the main form of expression for the majority of our ancestors over centuries: peasants, artisans, farm workers, miners, spinners and weavers, seafarers, tradespeople and tinkers, roving actors and musicians, grooms and maidservants – all sang of their experiences at love and work, fairs, harvests and seasonal rituals, and the impact of wars and food shortages. Their songs speak straight to my heart and I can feel the feelings, imagine the scene and find myself connected to a thread of experience that comes to me through many past lives.

I am not a folklorist or a scholar, but I hope to be an artist and to bear witness to the artistry of the common people who have gone before. It is their struggles, hardships and sacrifices in the pre-industrial countryside and in the industrial towns that created the possibility of a basic standard of living for all, and we forget this debt at our peril. Our post-industrial technological society has cut us off from our connections with nature and with the past, severing our cultural roots. I am not advocating a return to traditional ways of life, but I am saying that for us to know our cultural heritage, to know how the common people who were our ancestors lived, thought, despaired, hoped and fought, is important.

Mac was the undisputed leader of our group and we missed him sorely when he went off to do his National Service in 1957. After his demob in 1959 we set about extending our repertoire with renewed vigour, very much influenced by the work of Pete Seeger and the Weavers. By the early 1960s we gave our group the new name of the Ceilidh Singers. In those days hardly anyone knew how to pronounce the Celtic-influenced name 'ceilidh' (*kaylee*), let alone what it meant: a gathering where songs are sung, stories told and dances danced. The new name indicated our orientation towards folk music, though our repertoire was still drawn from a wide field – songs from North America, Britain and Ireland, spiced with the odd African chant and Israeli round. We were eclectic in the extreme, which suited the wide range of contexts in which we played.

We sang regularly at a small folk club we had started ourselves in the upstairs room of a pub in Hoddesdon. By now, there were several other clubs of this kind in Hertford-shire and we sometimes got invited to sing in these, as well as at church functions, old people's events, social events for the handicapped, student parties and fund-raising concerts for famine and refugee relief.

At this point we encountered a provocative demand from the leaders of the burgeoning British Folk Revival. They claimed it was important not to allow ourselves to be culturally colonized, especially from across the Atlantic, and to research and sing songs from our own culture. This led to heated discussions, excited argument and a growing sense that we were becoming part of a movement that could become a real cultural challenge to the market place.

Our repertoire changed in response to this demand. We quickly discovered a wealth of British songs and ballads which were every bit as enjoyable and moving to sing as those from the States. What was more, I found a new kind of satisfaction in singing songs that had come to us from our ancestors. Being of working-class origin – all the women of my very large family were in service two generations back – I found it strangely moving to reflect that the songs I was now learning might well have been sung by my own great-grandmother, telling of her experiences, or possibly her grandmother's. Though I do sometimes perform songs from other parts of the world, most of my repertoire still has its roots somewhere in these islands.

Life and Love, Work and Song

Chapter 4

Six months after my diagnosis at Moorfields, I had an operation for the raised intraocular pressure (glaucoma) in my left eye. I was then 17. For a while afterwards the eye seemed to be holding its own, but this intervention was not a long-term success. At the end of the year I went into Moorfields' residential clinic in Highgate for about four months' intensive in-patient care, hoping for an improvement, but the condition had been there for too long and it had too solid a hold. All the specialist could achieve was to stabilize it, so that for a while it didn't get any worse.

I left the clinic in May 1959 and my parents took me to Pennygyred in North Wales for a holiday. The weather was wonderful. My brother Tony and his girlfriend of the time came with us, as did my boyfriend Mike Wilkinson. It should have been idyllic, but I kept having temper tantrums on the slightest pretext and felt quite out of control. I couldn't understand it, thinking that I should be wildly happy to be out of hospital in that beautiful part of the world with my dear ones. Looking back now, I realize that the temper tantrums must have been an expression of the profound disappointment which I couldn't allow myself to articulate consciously. What I was trying not to face was the seriousness of the eye conditions and the hospital's failure to restore any of my lost vision. I still didn't realize, then, that the conditions would lead to much more severe sight loss and the possibility of blindness.

Over the year that followed I believe I gradually came to terms with my situation. I could still see well enough to draw, which was one of the main joys of my life, and to go about independently. The crucial problem, now that I could barely see well enough to read, was in looking for employment. At this point the Youth Employment Service and the

Disablement Resettlement Officer came into the picture in ways which still find hard to credit.

The Youth Employment Officer, a young woman, asked me what I was interested in. With the difficulties I had in reading, all the things that interested me and could lead to employment got knocked on the head rather fast. I made one suggestion which, with hindsight, I still think was a sensible one: that I should work as a kennelmaid in one of the guide dog training establishments. I had a long-term idea of training as a Home Teacher for the Blind, but knew I wouldn't be allowed to start this until I was at least 20. The idea of filling in the time as a kennelmaid with guide dogs felt like a realistic suggestion, but the Employment Officer's reaction was to come up with one or two quite different suggestions, and say, 'Go away and think about it. You can come back and see me when you've got this idea of working with doggies out of your head!'

I was then referred to the Disablement Resettlement Officer at the Labour Exchange, who could only suggest that I go and be trained as a capstan lathe operator! I didn't know what a capstan lathe operator was. When I found out, I realized that he couldn't have hit on anything less appropriate. I knew that whatever I was going to end up doing, I would be happier for the interim to remain broke, painting and potting (I was doing evening classes in pottery), singing, doing some voluntary work with the local blind club and going up to London once a week to see the old deaf and blind woman we called Gran.

We were having a stunningly beautiful summer. Mum and I cycled to the swimming pool nearly every day and sat reading under the magnolia tree on the lawn. We had a good time and I learnt to live my life as it came, day by day, waiting for the day when I would be old enough to train.

On a cool spring morning in 1962, Mum and I travelled up to London for my selection interview for training as a Home Teacher for the Blind. At the headquarters of the Southern

Region Association for the Blind we juddered up to the fifth floor in a rattling old lift.

As we scampered out, we met a puffing figure who was just reaching the landing via the stairs. There was barely room for three of us, so instant contact with Sal Bayley was inevitable.

'Are you here for the interviews?' she gasped.

I said I was and she laughed with evident relief. 'Thank heavens! I was scared they would all be from the tweeds and brogues brigade!'

Sal was wearing a blue coat which set off her straight platinum blonde hair to striking effect. During the selection procedure we discovered that we had similar responses to the questions we were asked. By the end of the morning we had established a sense of camaraderie which has remained with us, give or take the odd hiccup, for 28 years.

On hearing that we had been accepted for the course, Sal and I wrote to one another and decided to share a flat. I was 21 and ready to leave home: the transition felt calm and easy and I was excited to be moving to London. We set ourselves up in an unlovely bedsit near Clapham Common with a few kitchen implements from home, supplemented by purchases from Woolworths and Katharine Whitehorn's *Cooking in a Bedsitter*. Our course was housed in another dreary building overlooking the grounds of Lambeth Palace. We struggled with Braille, a simpler reading system called Moon and a range of crafts, as well as learning about the history and practice of Blind Welfare. When it all got too much, we would take refuge in The Windmill pub on Clapham Common.

Among our fellow students, Sal and I had the reputation of being 'Bohemian'. We weren't particularly outrageous, but we did wear black tights and Spanish ponchos and talk about the meaning of life. We also supported CND and its stance at the time of the Cuban missile crisis. Maybe these were quite radical things to be doing, but I also feel the reaction from our fellow students says a lot about the rather staid candidates chosen for the course.

Luckily, this was not my whole life. I was still singing with the group at weekends and we were occasionally invited to perform further afield, even in London. A circuit of folk clubs was becoming established and we sang regularly at St Albans and Harlow as well as our club in Hoddesdon. So I had the continuity of singing alongside my new life as a student in London. Our first London booking was at the Troubadour in Earl's Court. Standing in the dimly lit, smoky cellar surrounded by a relatively sophisticated London audience felt very glamorous, and I was thrilled to be written up in the *Melody Maker* by the doyen of folk journalists, Eric Winter.

Eric took it upon himself to encourage the Ceilidh Singers and I got to know the exciting world of the London 'folk scene'. He was a very sociable man with a passion for people, politics and singing. I spent a lot of time at his flat in Cricklewood, where he and his wife Audrey were always surrounded by friends and colleagues, singing, telling stories and discussing politics while the kids ran in and out, being loud and boisterous.

Then, to my eternal delight, Eric invited us to a party in the great Pete Seeger's honour. We saw Pete's concert at the Albert Hall – it was spellbinding, the first time I had seen one person speak to thousands as if they were a handful of friends round a camp fire. We sang at his behest, held our breath together, laughed and cried together.

It was like a dream come true to be at a party in Pete's honour. I remember sitting on the floor of a wood-panelled room somewhere in North London, singing 'Abiyoyo' and joining Pete in the actions of 'We're Going on a Bear Hunt'. And I clearly remember Dominic Behan standing in the middle of the room, flies gaping drunkenly open, and singing, oh so passionately, 'The old triangle, it goes jingle jangle, All along the banks of the Royal Canal' (dreaming, no doubt, of Ireland united and free).

When Sal and I needed a break from endless craft work and memorizing the details of Blind Welfare legislation, we would often visit a folk club. I can't remember at which club we came across Louis Killen, but I do know that it was an upstairs loft and that he sang magnificently.

Lou was rightly considered one of the greatest interpreters of the British tradition. Coming from Tyneside, he had a wealth of songs from the Northeast as well as many of the 'big ballads' and some contemporary songs. Lou singing 'Sally Free and Easy' would always send shivers down my spine. He played guitar, banjo and concertina, was never flashy or macho in his presentation, but communicated an energy which made the song more important than him. He was extremely attractive, aged around 30 and currently unattached. There was this strange thing called sexual attraction between us – one of life's mysteries, not so readily under our control as other elements when it comes to making rational choices. Given all these factors, it was unlikely that I would say no when he offered me a lift home!

We were happy to discover that we were both booked to sing at an event on the old sailing ship, the *Cutty Sark*, about a week later. I had the stomach collywobbles and butterflies throughout the intervening days until, at last, Saturday arrived, the sun shone and new love blossomed amongst the rails and riggings!

Up to this meeting I had certainly sung with passion and was clearly able to move an audience, but at that point Lou started to challenge me to go a step further. He earned his living mostly by singing for folk clubs and festivals and there were times when I was able to join him and sing a few duets. To be given this opportunity was a greater challenge than I had at first realized. Lou was a fine, instinctive singer, but he also took pains to think about phrasing, timing, pitching, ornamenting and all the subtle nuances that make for great interpretations of song. Learning to sing with him made me aware of aspects of singing that I hadn't met up to this point. He showed me new ways of making a song come alive, teasing out the relationship between words and melody. I learnt to phrase sung words as close to the spoken rhythm as possible.

I also learnt the importance of listening to traditional

singers, with their crucial stylistic manners. I learnt that content, style and form all developed organically and cannot be divorced. Finding how a tune and text could be made to work, word by word, line by line and verse by verse became like the unravelling of a mystery story.

Working in this way was enjoyable: it enriched my awareness and skills. But I was less happy when Lou pointed out my shortcomings. 'You either need to take your voice up and harden it or down and harden it.'

As with any young lover, I wanted him to accept me, my voice, my singing, unconditionally, so his criticisms left a little bruising on my heart. But I recognized that what he was saying was essentially true. So I listened to Jeanie Robertson, Isobel Sutherland, Belle Stewart, Rae Fisher, Sarah Makem and others. Then I tried imitating some of their vocal qualities. Listening intently to the sound of my voice in turn about with what I heard, I noticed that it had a more rounded, plummy sound than these traditional singers. It wasn't a question of taking it 'up' or 'down', but of giving it a more sinewy, edgey quality. But how? I imitated and I imitated again – and suddenly, there it was! A totally new sound, it was immensely exhilarating.

At the time I couldn't articulate the difference in words: I could only feel and hear that it was entirely different from the sound I was used to making when I sang. I knew immediately that this voice was all of a piece with the quality of traditional songs and ballads. I was also excitingly aware that it was going to open up more dramatic power in my singing.

I know now that what I had discovered was what is known in most formal and classical styles of singing as the 'chest' voice (though I prefer to use the term 'basic' voice in relation to traditional singing). It is a way of using the voice which comes naturally to children in playgrounds with their chanting of 'Yeah, yeah, yeh-yeah, yeah!' but which in western cultures we are trained out of when we are taught to 'sing'.

For a while it was terrifying because even on stage I couldn't be sure which quality was going to emerge from my mouth! I was also using too much tension in the throat to produce the result I wanted, and I found that my voice became tired at the end of every concert.

It was another year before I inadvertently discovered how to create the desired sound without strain. I was on a train going to Stoke-on-Trent to sing at a very lively folk club when, to my horror, I began to feel my throat getting that sore, knife-edge feeling that often comes at the start of a cold. It got worse, but I somehow found a way of 'placing' the voice that gave me the sound without putting a strain on my larynx – in fact, the sound was stronger and more resonant. Once the cold was over I went back to experimenting, to find out what had made this possible. It wasn't until many years later that I found ways to describe and pass on this process, which is one of the essential components of my voice workshops.

In the spring and early summer of 1963 I began to travel further afield with Lou at weekends and to be invited back to a number of clubs in my own right. I remember one club organizer asking 'What is your club fee?' I suppose this marks my entrance into professional singing. I had no idea what my fee was, so I hastily mentioned a figure somewhere around half of Lou's, which seemed commensurate with my experience and was about two-thirds of my weekly student grant. It felt extraordinary to be offered money to do something I loved doing with the chance to travel thrown into the bargain!

Chapter 5

Sal and I qualified as Social Workers for the Blind in 1963. We spent the summer hitchhiking around Greece before taking up jobs with Middlesex County Council, Sal in the Mill Hill area and me dividing my time between the Willesden and Harrow offices.

My two areas were strikingly different. The Harrow area was suburban and I never could identify either with the office or with the locality. I felt much more at home in the down-at-heel Willesden area, where I worked three days in the week. For all the dingy, overpopulated streets and the bad housing, I felt easier with the people there: maybe their poverty made them less conventional, but more than anything I think it was because the area still had a genuine sense of community.

My job was to visit those registered blind or partially sighted and to provide them with appropriate services, which might include kitchen aids, white canes for those who ventured out, talking books and arrangements for outings and holidays, as well as encouraging people to apply for the additional pension benefits they were entitled to. In practice, friendly and regular visiting seemed to be the most valuable part of the work. I could listen for hours to old men and women telling of days before the turn of the century when ox carts rolled up the A5 and pigeon racing was a regular sport.

In my first six months I zealously pressed on people every service they were entitled to. However, when holidays were cancelled at the last minute and talking books left gathering dust in corners, it slowly dawned on me that I was responding to my anxieties, not theirs. This is possibly the most essential realization that anyone in the helping professions can have.

This was when I met Mrs Duberry. She was referred from Harrow Road Hospital as recently registered blind. I rang the doorbell of the house in a dilapidated Victorian terrace and the door was opened by a woman of 83 with a finely-chiselled face and eyes bright and sparkling as you'd see on an 18-year-old in love.

'Mrs Duberry?' I inquired, pronouncing the name carefully.

'That's me, love – Mrs Dubry,' she said with a broad grin and an equally broad London accent.

Over the next two years I was to visit her almost every week. Her husband was in the final stages of muscular dystrophy and was in bed, doubly incontinent. The nurse came every day to wash and change him and the laundry service came regularly too, but she often needed to wash sheets herself. Her little first-floor landing kitchen would be festooned with sheets, the oven door open to provide the only heating. Over the years of visiting and collecting her pension when the weather made it too dangerous for her to venture out, I got to know one of the most wonderful women I've ever known with one of the toughest lives.

As a young teenager she had wanted to be a nurse, but her soldier father wouldn't hear of it, saying there was no point in wasting money to keep a girl at school. At 14 she became a lower chambermaid to the family of a lord who had houses both in London and in the country. One day when she was cleaning out the baths the lord raped her. After the family returned from spending the summer in the country, it became obvious that she was pregnant. She was turned out of the house around Christmas time with nothing but her meagre belongings in a little hamper. She wandered off and found herself at Marble Arch where there was a stand selling tea. A soldier offered to buy her a cup and at this unexpected kindness she broke down and told him her story. He said he was on leave visiting his mother in Purley and invited her to go with him, which she did. When he came out of the army they were married and set up a signwriting business. For a while they were quite prosperous. He drank and beat her periodically, but because she felt a sense of loyalty and gratitude to him for 'saving' her, she stayed with him, even though there was no love left. By the time he fell ill there was no money left either. This was their unenviable situation when her sight became poor and I arrived to visit her as 'the lady from the Welfare'.

Mrs Duberry's indefatigable spirit energized and inspired me. I looked forward to visiting her and knew this was mutual. I couldn't blame others who in similar circumstances were depressed and complaining, but people like Mrs Duberry were a monument to the human spirit.

Sal and I found a first-floor flat in an old red brick house in Rondu Road, Cricklewood, with a wilderness of a garden at the back. I had plans to tame the four-foot-high grass so we could sit outdoors in the summer, but I hadn't bargained on a development in my life which was to take over all the spare time and energy I had.

The Ceilidh Singers had disbanded, due to pressures of work and personal commitments, but through Lou I had begun to meet influential figures in the folk scene, including Bert Lloyd (A L Lloyd on the jackets of his books and records) and Ewan MacColl. Ewan had been active in political theatre since the 1930s and was one of the founders of Theatre Union. He was married to Joan Littlewood in the 1940s and they had set up Theatre Workshop together. When he and Joan separated, Ewan put most of his stupendous energy into singing and writing songs. He and Bert founded the Ballads and Blues Club, which later changed its name to the Singers Club. Then he co-created the Radio Ballads with Peggy Seeger and the BBC producer Charles Parker. But despite one of the Radio Ballads winning the Italia Prize, the BBC withdrew their financial support and these large-scale programmes ceased to be viable.

Ewan then decided to create an independent group whose purpose would be to study the nature and forms of traditional song, to generate new songs and to create projects both for recording and for the theatre. Ewan had asked Lou if he would join such a group, but for a variety of reasons he decided not to. However, in the early summer of 1964 Lou put it to me that such a group would give me an opportunity to carry on with my explorations. Why didn't I join?

I can't actually recall the moment of dialling the famous Ewan MacColl and Peggy Seeger to ask if there was any chance of my joining the group, but it must have been scary. However, they were kind and encouraging, and invited me to tea on a Saturday afternoon. I must have impressed them at least with my seriousness, as I was invited to join the group after the summer break.

So, that autumn, I joined the little team that met on Platform 3 at Victoria station to travel down to Ewan and Peggy's in Beckenham. Among them I found Jim Bassett (also from the Ceilidh Singers), Brian Pearson (of the St Albans Folk Club), Sandra Kerr, John Faulkner and Jim O'Connor. There were about ten of us that Tuesday evening in Ewan and Peggy's working room, which was lined with books, records and instruments. The very thought of all that music and information excited me.

Ewan outlined his theory that once upon a time bardic schools had trained apprentices in the traditional arts, and said this was the model he would like us to adopt. By now he was in his late forties. He had an immensely forceful personality with an emphatic way of speaking which gave him an air of great authority. He appeared to have an encyclopaedic knowledge of politics, philosophy, anthropology, theatre and traditional song. He had learnt many of the songs he sang from his parents: classical ballads from Betsy, his mother, vaudeville and city songs from his father.

Peggy, still in her early thirties, was vivacious and attractive with a driving energy that wouldn't let her be still. She would sit by Ewan while he expounded his ideas, always with a piece of crochet or needlework in her quick-moving fingers, until she was required to take up one of her many instruments to play and sing. Then we would realize what a gifted and knowledgeable woman she was.

As part of our apprenticeship on that first evening Ewan played us some examples of vocal styles from different traditions. The ones I remember best were a song from

Azerbaijan, with singing skilled enough to rival the best operatic tenor; a working song from a woman in India and another working song from women in the Hebrides, all showing the uncanny similarities in style which are found in working songs the world over. At the time I had no idea how profoundly these were to influence my later life.

On subsequent Tuesday evenings, for the next six years, one coach of the train from Victoria to Beckenham would be alive with stimulating conversation about singers we had heard, records we had come across, songs we had researched and ideas generated by the sessions with Ewan and Peggy, all spiced with a good deal of laughter and hilarity.

At our gatherings we listened to singers from different parts of Britain and Ireland, observing their individual and regional stylistic elements; we looked at the nature of instrumental accompaniment; we thought about the ways in which the idioms of working–class dialect and the vernacular varied from the language of standard English or 'received pronunciation'. Sometimes one person would present, say, a half-hour 'set' of songs with introductions he or she might use in a folk club and the group would offer useful criticism.

A matter of months after I joined, Charles Parker was asked about the group and its work in a radio interview. At that point we had no name and the interviewer pressed Charles to suggest one. The name he came up with was 'The Critics Group', arising out of just one aspect of our work together. The name stuck and for years it was a millstone. Much as I loved and respected Charles, I cursed him for inventing that one. Ewan already had a reputation for arrogance among people who disagreed with his ideas or simply found it hard to relate to him in person. Now the name of the group could be construed by others in the folk revival as implying that we were setting ourselves up as critics and custodians of the 'correct' criteria.

At this stage in my life I was still somewhere on the fringes of the radical theology movement, believing in something closer to Shaw's 'vital force' than any personal God figure.

My beliefs contained a strong desire for social justice and a fairer distribution of the world's resources, together with moral outrage at the strong and powerful crushing the weak and poor. What I lacked was any kind of economic or historical analysis to back my gut feelings. I was therefore ripe for the political education which was part and parcel of working with Ewan and the group.

Writing this 25 years on and with other influences, particularly the Women's Movement, having taken precedence since that time, I remain grateful for the chance I had then to explore and debate political and economic ideas. During those first months Ewan handed us all reading lists, ranging widely over anthropology, social history, political thought, plays and drama theory, and taking in works on folk song and traditional culture. It was a mind-boggling list, even for a speed reader. Ewan, in his exaggerated fashion, assured us that we could not consider ourselves serious, educated people if we hadn't read every book on the list.

At this point I could read only by holding the page very close to my left eye, managing to see about two words at a time. It was incredibly difficult to hold up a heavy book and crane over it so as to get the light falling on the page and line up my limited field of vision. I swear I have a permanent crick in my neck from all the reading I did in this manner, yet there were scores of books I never got around to. My suspicion is that I was not the only one.

A number of us from the Critics Group took part in a series of radio documentaries called 'Landmarks'. Each programme tackled a different social theme. My programme was about housing, and here I met the producer, Alasdair Clayre. Alasdair was one of the most brilliant and eccentric people I have ever known. Educated at Winchester and Oxford, he had been made the youngest ever Fellow of All Souls. He was a true polymath: his first degree was in English and his second in Politics, Philosophy and Economics. When I met him he was writing poems and songs and flirting with an offshoot of Scientology called 'The Process'. Later he worked as an

Open University producer. He killed himself in the seventies. It transpired he had had a terminal illness and, being who he was, couldn't face losing his remarkable abilities.

I remember the youthful Alasdair of 1964, given to wild enthusiasm and literally bobbing up and down as he talked, breathless with the speed at which ideas came to him. I was surprised and flattered that he seemed to find me interesting company. Undoubtedly there was an element of sexual attraction, but being Alasdair it could never be straightforward. Though we holidayed and toured together, it was never a 'consummated' romance.

Alasdair introduced me to a guitarist friend of his, Michael Jessett, who was arranging some of his songs. He wanted me to sing some of them and Michael to accompany me. Michael was also extraordinary. He was adopted and had been brought up on a working-class estate in North London. There had been nothing in his upbringing to encourage him towards music. After school he had trained as an RAF pilot but just before his graduation, so he told me, 'I was flying back to base feeling proud of my achievements when I flew over a bomber parked in the runway. It struck me like a thunderbolt that what I was ultimately trained for was to fly one of those things and drop, if ordered to, bombs. I must have thought about it before, but this time it was different. I simply knew I wasn't prepared to do this. So I managed to get out.'

When I met Michael he was teaching guitar at the Royal College of Music and gaining a reputation both as a teacher and as a recitalist. He had no formal training and, incredibly, he had stiff finger joints. He lived in a flat just off Gloucester Road, with a large room that he both worked and slept in, furnished with exquisite taste, though not expensively – simple cottage Chippendale chairs and a carved bed surround. It looked out on one of those large gardens to which only an elite handful of people in the block had access. Best of all, he had a Siamese cat called Mischa whom I grew to love dearly.

I was spending so much time at Michael's that by the

middle of the summer he suggested that I stay there for a while. I moved my belongings into his spare room, but I don't think I slept there once. In a matter of weeks I was besottedly in love with him.

In 1965 the Middlesex County Council ceased to exist and the newly formed London Borough of Brent decided only to employ full-time social workers, so I lost my part-time job in Blind Welfare. I could have applied for a full-time job, but I wanted more time to develop my singing so I decided to take the risk of being jobless and hoped that enough singing work would come my way to support my modest lifestyle.

In the spring I was immensely flattered to be invited to take part in a programme called 'Poets in Public' at the Edinburgh Festival. Ted Hughes, John Betjeman, Stevie Smith, Dannie Abse, George Barker, George MacBeth, Norman MacCaig, Hugh MacDiarmid and others were reading, and the organisers feared that so much reading might be difficult for the audience. So I was hired as an unaccompanied singing voice to punctuate the poetry. Then Michael got excited by the prospect and offered to do some accompaniments and, if the poets were willing, some settings of their poems. In this way three new settings came into existence: Peter Porter's 'The Ballad of Johnny Comino', Hugh MacDiarmid's 'Wha's the Bride?' and John Betjeman's 'The Night Club Hostess'.

The Festival was a great success. Betjeman was delighted with the setting of his poem and I received a hug and a kiss! Stevie Smith also took part in the Festival. She was my ideal of a wonderful witch with that delicious, quirky sense of humour and her way of half speaking, half chanting her poems, her little pointed face framed with straight, rather straggly hair. I fell in love with her both times I worked with her.

David Frost was doing a late-night TV show from the Festival Club and on one evening Michael and I were invited on to the show to do a song. Mortifyingly, I made a horrible mistake and on live television too. I simply missed out a chorus of 'Johnny I Hardly Knew You'. It mattered particularly because Michael had arranged the song with a special tuning that created a feeling of distant marching drums. His solo guitar bit got completely cut out by my omission. He was attentive enough to cover up, so no one but us knew that I 'blew it', but I felt suicidal afterwards. I had been unprofessional enough to get something wrong and rob Michael of his stunning guitar solo. The fact that he was the only person who knew this was no comfort. He was the one who mattered! The traffic roared along the main street outside the Freemasons' Hall and I was aware of a temptation to throw myself under some oncoming vehicle and end my shame and failure. It was, I think, the first and last time I have felt suicidal because of a mistake on stage. It probably had much more to do with an impending fear that my affair with Michael was not going to develop as I wanted and that this episode would hasten its end.

Around that time, two record companies expressed an interest in making a record of Michael and me. We went to discuss this but talk of bland TV music shows, little black dresses for me, and renaming us 'Frankie and Mickie' put us off entirely. We objected and left with a clear impression that if we were not prepared to play by the rules, they were not interested in us. We never heard from them again, but I never regretted that stance.

That week at the Edinburgh Festival was probably the most heady period of my life. By certain standards it could be viewed as the pinnacle of my career, in terms of prestige and fame and the status of the people I was working with. One day a friendly assistant of George MacBeth's remarked, 'Frankie, you'll have so many offers of work after this that you won't know which ones to take up!'

There is also a saying, 'Blessed is she who has no expectations, for she shall not be disappointed!' I received not one single offer as a result of 'Poets in Public'.

After we returned to London, just as I had feared, Michael said he wasn't happy for me to go on living with him. I began to look for a bedsitting room and finished up with a room overlooking the District Line not far from Michael's.

I was now living alone for the first time in my life and it wasn't an easy time. I had a few folk club bookings, but after the excitement of the summer, life was suddenly rather bleak. It was also quite possible that I might run out of money. I missed Mischa and the sunlight dappling the bed as the sun rose behind the trees outside Michael's window. I had lain in bed on warm summer evenings with the windows wide open, the sound of rustling leaves accompanying Bach preludes as Michael practised late into the night. I missed the excitement of wondering who it might be when the doorbell rang – one day it had been his friend Julian Bream, who had just collected a new guitar from the maker and popped round to compare it with one of Michael's, made by the same man. It was like being in heaven, all three of us sitting on the bed, as they swapped guitars and set up improvisations around great old jazz classics.

Most of all, of course, I missed Michael. We still saw quite a bit of each other and had a few engagements together, but my dreams of taking up permanent residence in his heart and home were at an end. My first depression of any length descended. It deepened after I learnt that Michael was smitten by one of his young guitar pupils from the College. She was blonde and ethereally beautiful. My Capricorn earthiness has never been able to compete with this kind of woman and I knew when I was beaten. As is often the way, he would come to me for comfort when she was being too mysterious and distant. I would listen and console him with my aching heart, lovesick fool that I was, and long for a return to the past.

I had practical problems, too. I was behind with the rent, which was out of character for me. So, when my old boss, who was now Chief Welfare Officer for the London Borough of Hillingdon, phoned and offered me a part-time job as a welfare officer for the blind, I accepted. This return to social work was not what I had hoped for. At the same time, somewhere deep down, I realised I wasn't quite ready to be a full-time singer.

When the Critics Group reassembled after the summer, Ewan presented us with the idea of doing a full-length show after Christmas, based on the medieval notion of the Festival of Fools. Rehearsals started in earnest in early November. For two months we met in New Merlin's Cave, the pub in whose back room the Singers Club met every week. It was bitterly cold and unlovely, but Ewan was dedicated to bringing song and theatre to the people and unlovely pubs were where the people went.

It was exciting to see the show taking shape, weaving together the events of the past year with folklore and the customs of each month. Our main problem was Ewan's tendency to overwrite. He had some glorious ideas and wrote well, but half the scenes would have been improved by pruning. Ironically, we discovered that the founder of the Critics Group couldn't bear criticism of himself: we tried with the utmost diplomacy to suggest cuts to tighten up the show, but I can't recall one word ever being removed as a result.

I enjoyed the intensity of working towards a production and the adrenalin rush that got us through two weeks of nightly performances. The beginning always had Brian Pearson as Narrator telling us of the European custom around New Year by which slaves were served by their masters, orgies were allowed in churches and the Lord of Misrule conducted revels in which 'the world was turned upside down'. We sang wassailing songs, generating a feeling of celebration. Then 'The blackest month of all the year is the month of Janiveer.' Bang! We would be off into some scene or sketch of a political event of the previous January, introduced by a newspaper clipping of the time.

When the frenetic two weeks of the first show came to an end, we were into 1966 with my 25th birthday looming. My little bedsit could be kept warm with a fire, but after Michael's lovely flat I missed the sun: it never reached my window in winter. This detail seemed to mirror my lovelorn life. Sal married Jim O'Connor of the Critics Group in late February and moved to Turnham Green, not far away, but this only served to point up my unrequited misery. She remained a close friend, but setting up a home and working in a full-time job understandably left her little time to spare. I still saw quite a lot of Michael, though I knew this wasn't helping me to 'get over' him. I just found it impossible to deny myself the chance of seeing him when he invited me.

This period, lonely and miserable as it was, taught me one of the most important lessons of my life. I kept expecting to find others who would understand and share my distress. This is not in itself an unhealthy desire, but it was unrealistic to expect someone else to be as concerned and absorbed in my feelings as I was. One day in early spring as I was walking along Courtfield Road it dawned on me that I was never going to find this, nor should I. I suppose this was the moment I came to terms with being alone. It is not an easy realization, but with it comes a tremendous feeling of relief and release. From that day I began to feel less devastated by my feelings about Michael. I even began to enjoy going out with other men in a way that I hadn't for nearly a year. There have been occasions since then when I have been lonely, but since that day I have always been able to accept that existential fact of aloneness. I can still experience real understanding and communion with others, but I believe this is much more likely to happen when I am not seeking a degree of involvement and investment in my unique inner life that makes unrealistic demands on another person.

That spring afternoon, after this moment of realization, the sky was suddenly more blue, the birds sang more sweetly and the desperation that had been my haunting companion for months slipped away. Nevertheless, that summer plunged me into two quite painful relationships. The first ended promptly when, thinking it would be a delightful surprise for my then boyfriend (who was spending the weekend in my room), I travelled home through the early hours of the morning from a folk club in the Midlands to find him there with another woman. I have no reason to believe any other men have cheated or deceived me; in this I feel lucky, but I also have a pretty clear instinct about who is trustworthy and who is not. That summer, however, my neediness was probably obscuring my judgement. At three that morning I was weeping and screaming as I told them to get out. It was some compensation that soon after this incident they got married. At least I had not been deceived for a one-night stand!

My second affair that summer taught me a painful, permanent lesson. In late August I had joined a group planning a holiday in Albania. The group, mostly ex-Communist Youth League with a sprinkling of oddities like myself, had a number of meetings before the trip to familiarize ourselves with recent Albanian history. Among them was a young man called Brian Byrne, also a member of the Critics Group and a fine, passionate singer of his native Irish songs. Our relationship began during the meetings.

As we spent more time together, Brian talked to me about his background. His mother and her many children had been so poor, they had lived in a deserted army barracks in Dublin, and in childhood he had often known real hunger. He also had a passion for literature and philosophy, and would pace up and down my little sunless room, telling me about Plato's ideas on the State. He would talk and talk and I could empathize with the way his experiences had brought about his intense commitment to the working class and revolutionary socialism.

Our trip took us through Europe and Yugoslavia to Budva, where we slept on the beach, feeling very Bohemian and romantic. After crossing the Albanian border in a violent storm we were made very welcome and found the people hospitable, eager to show us around their factories, sports stadiums, power plants and homes. As we travelled through the remoter parts of the mountainous north, I became aware of Brian's withdrawing from me, turning chilly and distant. One evening we found ourselves alone in a hotel bar and I asked him what was wrong. His answer was my lesson.

First he said that seeing the sparseness of people's lives in the northern villages had put him back in touch with his roots in poverty, driving a wedge between us as I came from a 'nice' middle-class background with no experience of that kind of suffering. But the real lesson followed when Brian said 'It's true, Frankie, that I've talked to you more, told you more about myself than anyone else ever – but don't think I'm going to thank you for this!'

Since that day I've consoled so many women who have been utterly bereft and bewildered at the emotional withdrawal of a man they felt had trusted them. 'But he told me so much about himself, poured out his soul!' I suspect that the withdrawal often happens because of the fear of emotional vulnerability which comes after they have 'poured out their souls'. I have to thank Brian for being sufficiently self-aware and open to let me know that this was at least part of what went wrong between us.

I returned from Albania sadder but wiser. After we got back Brian became quite dismissive of me. I must have been aware from my experience in social work that it was naïve to expect someone who had himself suffered to be more compassionate because of it, but we learn our personal lessons more slowly than our professional ones.

In September I went to a big demonstration on the London streets with the Vietnam Solidarity Front. As I had no one to go with, I set off on my own, trusting that I would find someone to guide me on the march. I was wandering by the Thames in the early evening sun, hoping that I was going towards the assembly point, when a soft voice with a north American accent said 'Is this the way to where the demonstration starts?' I replied that I hoped so and, seeing my white cane, he offered to help me.

Ron was a Canadian psychologist, recently arrived in England and planning to stay a year either working or studying. Being a socialist, it was natural that he should lend his support to such a demonstration. We ended the evening having supper with two friends of his, finding we all had a lot in common. I suggested to Ron that we do some sightseeing together, as I had lived in London for four years without visiting the Palace of Westminster or the Tower. Romance flourished and he moved in with me. Then he got a teaching job, which meant that we could afford to move somewhere more spacious. We found a palatial room on the sunny side of Courtfield Road with a big bay window facing south, all for seven pounds a week. On one wall was a mural of an Italian balustrade with trees spreading their branches into the blue sky. Another room had a carved wooden mantelpiece measuring eight feet across. With late afternoon sun pouring in and a view of the same gardens I had looked out on from Michael's flat, we felt ourselves to be in the lap of luxury.

Ron was a gentle soul with, I suspect, a tendency to mild depression. He coped with this by directing his anger against injustice and militarism: as there was no shortage of targets, it was an effective way of dealing with his feelings rather than taking them out on himself or me. His anger could suddenly turn into a cynicism which was untypical and sounded strange coming from a man with such gentle blue eyes. We made good comrades and companions.

When rehearsals began for the second Festival of Fools, Ron joined the cast. Though his accent was Canadian, he was inevitably cast as the hapless GI or Pentagon spokesman for this and the next production, parts which he accepted with good grace. The rehearsal schedule was gruelling and the room we worked in as cold and unlovely as ever, but it did ease things to share it all with my room-mate and lover.

The spring of 1967 was glorious. Although the gate into the well-tended gardens beside our flat was supposed to be padlocked, the caretakers whispered to us that they had positioned the chain so that it looked as if it was keeping the gate locked, but could be slipped off. This meant that on some weekdays we could surreptitiously make our way into the garden. The azaleas bloomed in a riot of pinks, reds and purples. I would take a book with me and sit there peering my way through it, word by word.

Ron introduced me to the writings of Abraham Maslow, and we became excited about R D Laing: those were the early days of the anti-psychiatry movement, which had its parallels in radical sociology and social work.

I remember one time when I was reading Laing in an empty compartment of a corridor train. A young man somewhat the worse for drink came in and sat down opposite, trying to start a conversation by asking me what I was reading. I was wearing my pebble-thick glasses, with my nose literally in a copy of *The Divided Self*. I replied without taking my head out of the book that I would be grateful to be left alone to get on with it. Undaunted by my obvious lack of interest or my unglamorous appearance, he moved over, sat next to me and tried to get his hand up my skirt.

I put my book down very calmly, took off my glasses, turned to face him so that his ear was a matter of inches from my mouth, and used my full vocal range of decibels to tell him to 'fuck off!'

I have never seen anyone look so startled or move so fast. By the time the guard and a member of the railway police peered in to see if I was all right, I was back with my book on the nature of the schizoid personality. They said they had heard a commotion and was I all right?

'I'm just fine,' I assured them, 'but I wouldn't be too sure about the idiot who tried to molest me.'

They ran off in pursuit, but as we had stopped at a station between whiles he must have got off. I've often wondered if he remembers the incident as clearly as I do!

My first appearance on record came about, as most of the best things in my life have done, through personal contact. I got to know Bert Lloyd (A L Lloyd, the international folklorist and song collector) around the folk festivals and had shared a platform with him on occasions. Bert was a director of Topic, a small but influential recording company, and when he was looking for a singer to take part with himself and Ann Briggs in a recording of amorous and erotic songs, he thought of me. 'The Bird in the Bush' came out in 1965. It was made and launched without fuss or hype, but it went far and I still rate it as one of my favourite records.

Bert Lloyd is not so well known as Ewan, but he was just as important in the Folk Revival. In his quiet, dedicated way he was a pioneering spirit with a lasting influence on many singers and groups. It was through my contact with him, above all others, that I was able to free myself from the notion of singing as a career and integrate it into my whole way of being.

Bert's way of just being with song had nothing to do with the pursuit of fame or recognition: it was simply a way of expressing his unique relationship with the world. It was not his encyclopaedic knowledge that made him the greatest influence of all on my singing: it was the way he sang. He had an ability to communicate both the 'story' of a song and some deeper, more mysterious meaning that lay below the surface. His singing had an emotional depth that spoke of a man who had been through great pain and was not afraid of passion, fear, love, lust, tenderness or savagery: they were all there, conveyed in his high, idiosyncratic voice. It could never be said that Bert had a 'good' voice: his pitch could be erratic and his breathing became difficult as he got older. But for me none of this mattered because the magic was always there.

Chapter 6

In the late sixties, Ewan and Peggy developed a good relationship with Argo Records, a subsidiary of Decca. The Critics Group had already made a series of books and records in conjunction with Macmillan Press called *Poetry and Song*, containing both traditional and new material. The first song I recorded for the series was 'Scarborough Fair', several years before the emasculated version produced by Simon and Garfunkel. How I loathe that version with its bland, sickly-sweet harmonies and reduced tune! I would hate it even if I had never recorded it.

We were very productive at that time. In 1966 and 1967 the men in the group researched and recorded sea shanties. The women decided that we would put together a pro-gramme for live performance and recording purposes exploring women's experience through song. We agreed that we would each go through our existing repertoire and pick out the songs that were specifically about women, and I found that a good two-thirds of my material fitted the description. Many of the songs spoke of desertion by lovers, often with the woman left pregnant or with a baby.

Oh happy's the girl who ne'er loved a man,
And easy can tie up her narrow waistband,
She's free from all sorrow and sad misery
Who never said 'My lover, you're welcome to me.'

and

So off he's gone and I wish him well
For to get married, this I hear tell,
My innocent babe I'll tend and care
And to his false vows I'll soon beware.

Sometimes she would be thrown over for another woman of a higher social status: 'And cruel was my own love who changed his mind for gold.' Sometimes the loss was due to the army recruiting officers who plied young men with drink and then gave them the King's shilling, thus recruiting them into the army:

> Last Monday he went into town
> And them red-coated fellows
> Enticed him in and made him drunk
> And he'd better gone to the gallows.

When men were wanted for the navy, the press gangs would physically drag them off:

> All things were quite silent, each mortal at rest,
> As me and my true love lay snug in one nest,
> When a bold set of ruffians they entered our cave
> And they forced my dear jewel to plough the salt wave.

Women might accompany their husbands and lovers to the wars:

> Come dress yourself all in your best and come along with
> me
> I'll take you to the wars my love in higher Germany.

It wasn't unknown for women to disguise themselves as sailors or soldiers, either to travel with or to seek their lovers or, in some cases, simply in search of adventure and travel themselves:

> When I was a young girl at the age of sixteen
> From my home I ran away to go and serve the Queen.
> The officer who enlisted me said 'You're a nice young
> man,
> I think you'll make a drummer, so just step this way young
> man.'

There were songs like 'Clear Away the Morning Dew' and 'The Crafty Maid's Policy' and 'Lovely Joan', which told of women using wit and wisdom to escape unwanted sexual advances. In 'The Outlandish Knight',

He's turned his face away from her
To view the leaves so green
She's catched him round his middle so small
And plunged him in the stream.

Lie there, lie there, you false-hearted man.
Lie there instead of me,
For if six pretty maids you have drownded there
The seventh one hath drownded thee.

Amongst the big ballads we found a large number that showed how the daughters of any family with pretensions to wealth or power were simply pawns in the business of increasing the status of the family. Ballads such as 'Bruton Town', 'Clerk Saunders', 'Tiftie's Bonnie Annie', 'Lady Diamond' and many, many others tell of a young woman falling in love with a servant and the inevitable tragedy that results:

Oh, Fyvie's lands are far and wide,
Fyvie's lands are bonnie,
But I wouldn't leave my own true love
For you and all your money.

After this defiance Tiftie's Bonnie Annie is murdered by her brother. This Scottish song is said to be based on a true incident, one among many such accounts.

When the group of us put our collective repertoires together we discovered we had a wealth of material that told us a great deal about the lives of our female ancestry. Peggy and Buff, another American member of the Group, had more songs about women working outside the home – 'Cotton Mills Girls' and others from earlier this century in the southern states. With a little searching we found a number of wonderful songs, especially from Ireland and Scotland, about working in the textile industry. We found songs about female 'highwaymen', a woman dying of syphilis and songs lamenting the housewife's lot.

This was some time before the spread of the Women's Movement in these islands. At that time we still perceived the issue of women's subjugation as part of class subjugation, so while we got angry about some of the issues raised by the songs, we analysed our anger within a socialist framework.

We had a wonderful time putting the programme together, discussing which songs to select and which to leave out. We found contemporary accounts of women's conditions to illuminate the sung material and presented the result at folk clubs up and down the country. Peggy, another Group member, Sandra and I made a record for Argo entitled *The Female Frolick*. It's a record I'm still proud to be part of.

At this point my sight was deteriorating very slowly. The uveitis and glaucoma were controlled by eye drops, so it was only the slow, inexorable forming of the cataract that was affecting my sight and I was not particularly depressed or fearful about it.

I talked a lot to Charles Parker about it. He drew me out when I talked about the dire state of most of the non-statutory Blind Welfare agencies, how in my experience those of us who had a visual impairment were stereotyped, and hence limited, by the very agencies who were supposed to encourage our independence. My first experience of this had been on a training placement with the Hertfordshire Society for the Blind when the director had greeted me with the words 'Good morning, Miss Armstrong. Welcome to Blind Welfare! I'm sure you'll have a most enjoyable time. I always find the blind such happy people!'

I talked to Charles about the way it affected us to be depicted on collecting boxes with dark glasses and pathetically outstretched hands, designed to tug heartstrings and open purses.

As a result of our conversations, Charles devised a radio programme which challenged the patronising attitudes of these charities. He interviewed many blind and partially sighted people and was appalled at what he found. There were (and still are) so many assumptions about what we could and could not do, especially when it came to employment. I had been young enough, stroppy enough and middle-class enough to disregard the 'capstan lathe' advice I was given at the Labour Exchange and make a way for myself. For those with appropriate A levels there was physiotherapy, for example, and there were some blind lawyers. But for the majority who lost their sight the options were incredibly narrow.

I wrote a song which I sang through the programme with the verses spread out between the interviews. It was based on my own experience and that of others I had known who had lost their sight.

The vision is blurring, the mist is swirling,
the fog never ends.
I'm faced with the question,
'When will the twilight descend?'

The dusk it has shrouded the faces around me,
the vision is dead.
The mind paints its image and pictures
from what's being said.

The friends that I had,
the people I knew,
all try to be kind,
but they're awkward and distant,
embarrassed because I'm blind.
They try to cajole me, they try to console me,
but to them I'm different, to them I'm somebody else.

I'll use every tool,
I'll learn every skill,

I'll find a new way to build a new life
so I'll walk by myself once again.
You try and you fumble, you cry and you stumble,
But it's better than being dependent on somebody else.

The touch of your hand,
the feel of your face,
my fingers can see
Providing the warmth and the contact
that bring you to me,
for you just accept me, don't try to protect me,
with you I can look to the future and fight for myself.

Charles had the capacity to fire people's smouldering resentments into full-blooded anger. By the time the programme went out there was a network of people just burning to do something about these conditions. This led to the formation of the Blind Integration Group (BIG), which made us heard for a while. As most of us were busy, active people, the group eventually lost momentum and faded out, but this was a crucial step in our moves towards self-definition and self-help.

In contrast to the buzz of ideas which made the late sixties so exciting, a tragic event brought the passing moment into sharp focus. This was the death of Brian Byrne from a rare form of leukaemia.

After he was admitted to St Stephen's Hospital in Fulham I visited him a number of times and found it desperately sad to see such a strong, vital man slowly wasting away. During one remission he came out and we spent an hour or so in an Irish bar near the hospital. He was more relaxed in such a setting and at one point said, 'Frankie, I realize I kicked you right in the teeth last year and you didn't deserve it.'

It was a courageous thing for him to say. Maybe when death is approaching we can escape old patterns. Brian wasn't someone who could apologize easily, especially around emotional matters. I am very grateful to him for having done this. It made it possible to say goodbye without 'unfinished business' between us. He was only in his thirties, a gifted, pained, passionate man, who at his best was a great singer of his nation's songs.

The Critics Group went on researching, making records and presenting feature evenings in the folk clubs. The themes we looked at included sea shanties and songs, women's songs and songs about London. Next on the list came Waterloo-Peterloo.

Each record had different permutations of researchers and singers. Waterloo-Peterloo was predominantly Dennis Turner, Brian Pearson, Terry Yarnell and myself. We decided to find out how songs reflected the life of ordinary people from about 1780 to 1830, the beginning of the Industrial Revolution. Our imaginations were fired. It was such a time of upheaval – industrial revolution, political revolution, agricultural revolution – with stormy events of the era mirrored in the songs people created. There is an almost breathless realization that the world is changing, never to return to its former order. There were the new urban slums, women's first employment in the early textile industry, farm labourers faced with cuts in their meagre wages and everywhere more wars and fences enclosing the common land on which people had relied to graze their animals and shoot the occasional rabbit or hare for the pot. Now people faced transportation to the new Australian colony for the shooting of a rabbit or a pheasant on the newly enclosed land.

It was during our work on this record that I really came to know Brian Pearson. He had separated from his wife Vicky in the summer of 1967. They had been together for as long as I could remember, founding the St Albans Folk Club, organizing the Tring events and renovating a beautiful old pub in St Albans where jazz and folk clubs held their sessions. Brian was a voracious reader with a rare ability to retain what he read. He could be eloquent and erudite on a wide range of subjects, from Roman Britain to geology, natural history and the social history and folklore of rural, pre-industrial England. He would deny this erudition: then as now, he was genuinely modest, recognizing that the more you know, the more you know that you don't know.

As my reading was so restricted, I found myself endlessly fascinated listening to Brian talk.

Ron and I were not actively falling out, but the initial spark had gone out of the relationship and as I was spending so much time on the Critics Group, we were predictably drifting apart. Ron enjoyed music, but was not obsessed with it like me. Nor was he at that time a walker, while I adored walking. Brian was fanatical about jazz and a passionate hill walker and climber.

One day, when my mother was driving me on to Cambridge to sing at the University folk club, I heard myself say, half-jokingly, 'Now where will I find a man who loves music, mountains, animals and folk songs and is politically sympathetic?'

As I came to the end of my question, the words 'Brian Pearson' simply popped into my head. Well, there was an interesting thought! It was a remarkably rational way to choose a romance.

Since Ron and I were still companionable, he moved out and found himself a room a few doors away. We went on spending time together and after one lunchtime visit to Hyde Park I encouraged him to go and visit a colleague of his from the Maudsley. Penny was a bright, intelligent woman and it was clear to me that Ron was very taken with her. Her romance of the day seemed to be in its final throes and I recall saying to Ron 'What have you got to lose?' In fact he had a great deal to gain.

Brian and I started living together, as so often happens, because of financial considerations. With my part-time income it was difficult for me to keep up the rent in Courtfield Road and I dreaded the prospect of another small, dark, cheap room. Brian had a room in St Albans but was hardly ever there. It made sense for him to move in with me so we could keep that sunny, spacious room. In one way, it was too early in the new, romantic stage of our relationship to have to deal with the emotional and practical vicissitudes of living together. Yet we weathered 17 years, supporting one another through tremendous changes; sharing joys, pains and fears; learning about trust and hurt; learning about dependence, independence and interdependence. Most of all we learnt how a strange, fragile flower called love can be tended and kept alive through thick and thin, through times together and times apart. It still flowers, though we are both with other partners, with no regrets.

Chapter 7

Brian moved in with me in the spring of 1968 – the spring of the Paris student and worker uprisings and the sit-in at the London School of Economics. This partly inspired us to apply for courses due to begin that September. We also wanted a change from the jobs we were doing. Brian decided to do a sociology degree and I a Certificate in Social Work.

With some trepidation, I wrote off for the application forms for three courses. The forms that arrived first were from the North West London Polytechnic, a course with a very good reputation. Nervously, excitedly, I began to fill them in. Peering through my magnifying specs, I read 'Name in full'. 'Frances Ann Armstrong', I wrote boldly. Then came the instruction 'Surname first'. I shrieked in fury and flung my glasses across the room. Brian glued them together while I sobbed that there was no point even trying, for what chance did I have if I couldn't even fill out the — forms?

Brian calmed me down and assured me that it wouldn't matter. Anyway, I would have to make it clear in my application that I was visually impaired and, 'If they hold this against you, then it's not the kind of course you want to be on anyway.' Since that moment, I have often found comfort in this thought: the kind of place that wouldn't want me is the kind of place that I wouldn't want either. It seems to have stood me in good stead.

So the autumn of 1968 had me simultaneously preparing for the next Festival of Fools and returning to full-time education at the North West London Polytechnic. I was struck with one interesting difference between being a student and being a performer: quite a different form of nerves hit me when introducing a paper for a tutorial or inter-jecting an idea in a class discussion. I could stand up on stage before hundreds of people, yet in these new situations I could feel myself reddening and my heart pounding. It was some time before I learnt to manage this without becoming anxious. As with so many things, it became easier with practice.

In retrospect, the placements I went on as part of my course are what stayed with me. We were sent out to get practical experience, backed up by supervisors. One of my supervisors was Marybelle, who had recently gone into analysis and asked me some probing questions about why I sang and how I chose songs to sing. One day she said 'D'you know, Frankie, it's as if you use singing as a self-analysis!' This made sense to me immediately and has helped me, both as an artist and as a person, to understand why I feel so deeply about many of the songs and why I remain excited about them.

In our summer holidays we were expected to undertake two residential placements of two weeks each. I asked for one of these to be the Henderson Hospital, an influential therapeutic community run along lines pioneered by Dr Maxwell Jones. His work began after the Second World War, when he was helping to rehabilitate disturbed and distressed soldiers, and was subsequently adopted by a few community psychiatric hospitals – in the case of the Henderson, for use with people often diagnosed as 'psycho-pathic'.

The aspect of the Henderson community that captured me was the sheer intensity of feelings and involvement in the day-to-day business of living. Apathy or trivia didn't get much of a look-in.

When they discovered that I sang, I was asked to give a concert. As I went about selecting which songs I would sing I became aware that many of the stories and emotions expressed in the songs, sometimes in a heightened or symbolic form, were very potent and present for many of those living at the hospital. I made a conscious decision to include songs about jealousy, savagery and violence as well as love songs and songs that addressed issues of the day.

I was quite nervous before the concert began, having no idea how an unaccompanied 'folk' singer would go down, since most of the audience would be rock fans. I was also aware of the responsibility of singing songs of such direct passions and imagery with no instrumental accompaniment, no barrier between me and the song or me and the hearers. If I sang a song about rape or abortion, there were probably people in the audience for whom this would stir deep, powerful personal feelings.

When I began to sing I realized that the songs were doing just this. The air was electric. The raw feelings and nerves touched were almost tangible. It was very exciting – the feeling of danger, the sparks flying, the sense of relief at the humorous items, the alert response to songs addressing the Vietnam war or the disaster of the slag heap that buried the children in Aberfan. The songs, like the sixties, were full of questioning. This concert was an experience against which I went on to measure the responses of 'normal' audiences. It made me somewhat frustrated and intolerant of 'soggy' audiences – those who do not wish to be disturbed or touched by the darker side of life.

The evening was a huge success. They asked me if I would go back and do another some weeks later and this time Brian and Jack Warshaw came with me. We found the space was prepared and decorated and refreshments arranged for the interval. The concert had the same vibrant atmosphere: Brian and Jack were struck, as I had been, by what a dangerous and wonderful audience these people made.

It was on this course that I had my first experience of a 'growth group' leader – I should say a male growth group leader, because in this instance the facilitator was on a none-too-cleverly disguised power trip. But later that year Brian and I went to our first series of Encounter Groups set up by Quaesitor and led by Richard Petersen. This was an experience of another order. I liked Richard immediately for his warmth and vulnerability. Two experiences were particularly moving and instructive and these, together with my earlier, not-so-happy experience, were of great value to me in my future group therapy work and voice workshops.

Not to contravene confidentiality, I will disguise the participants and some aspects of their stories.

At the first of our meetings it was noticeable that two of the men, 'Ben' and 'Dan', both in their early thirties and successful, disliked each other from the outset. Richard encouraged some well-contained 'acting out' of this antipathy. I'm now convinced that without this physicalization, the subsequent discoveries would not have occurred.

Ben became much more breathless and agitated than the 'reality' warranted: gradually his breath got shorter and more violent and he became flushed and sweaty. He had to take his jacket and tie off (he had come straight from work in neat suit) and then Richard led him through a sequence whereby he was able literally to 'get it off his chest'. As he became angrier, screaming and pounding a tennis racquet with enormous force on to a mattress, his breathing lowered from his upper chest to his belly. At last he crumpled into a sobbing heap and Richard gradually got him to voice what he was reliving in great internal and external detail. He was back to the age of five or six at the end of the war. His father had been an Army captain and had been away for the duration of the hostilities. He described his glamorous, beautiful mother and his fury and sense of abandonment on the return of this stranger who took away the hitherto exclusive love and attention of his mother. As Ben recovered his composure and came back to us in the circle, he looked at Dan. Both their faces and expressions had softened almost beyond recognition. Ben said, 'Of course, now I realize that Dan reminds me of how my father looked when he was young!'

Brian and I walked back to the tube with Ben, and though he was obviously shaken by the experience he said it was as if a weight were off his chest and shoulders. That night and subsequent evenings at Quaesitor I realized that hurt and anger were very closely related and that some people, like myself, become angry sometimes to cover up hurt, while others use hurt to cover up anger.

'Lily' seemed an unlikely candidate for the very physical

and imagistic type of therapy that Richard used. She was in her late fifties with the rather precise, prim manner of a seemingly conventional woman from the upper middle classes. I felt it must have taken courage for her to come to such an event. It became clear that she had tried conventional therapy, yoga and meditation in an attempt to relieve the tension and sleeplessness she had suffered from since the death of her husband some years before. He had been somewhat older than her and had died of a heart attack whilst they were making love. As well as the grief and the loss, Lily had been burdened by guilt, feeling that it was her fault for still being sexually active. This all came out after a seemingly unrelated exercise which affected Lily strongly.

Using the Gestalt technique of putting out two chairs, or in this case cushions, Richard suggested that Lily have a conversation with her dead husband, speaking from Cushion A as herself and moving to Cushion B to respond as him. What transpired was one of the most moving pieces of drama I have ever witnessed. Lily, in her floral dress with her prim, elegant manner, gave herself wholeheartedly to this two-way conversation, switching back and forth between the cushions, starting with self-reproach and paralysing guilt, till the voice of her husband emerged clearly telling her not to hold herself to blame. Towards the end, Lily's face had completely changed. The tension round her mouth and eyes had disappeared. When it was clear to her that the resolution had been reached, she burst into a cry of relief and literally somersaulted across both cushions.

We were all weeping. The intensity of her relief over being able, at long last, to let him go, was tangible. I asked her if I could sing her an old ballad, as it seemed to me she had undergone the same process that this ancient and widespread song speaks of.

THE UNQUIET GRAVE

Cold blows the wind tonight my love
And a few small drops of rain

I never had but one true love
And in greenwood he is lain.

I'll do as much for my true love
As any young girl may
I'll sit and mourn all on his grave
A twelve month and a day.

The twelve month and a day being past
The ghost began to speak.
'Who sits and mourns on my graveside
And who will not let me sleep?'

''Tis I my love sits by your grave
And I will not let you sleep.
I crave one kiss from your clay cold lips
And this is all I seek.'

'My lips are cold as clay, sweetheart,
My breath tastes earthy strong,
If you have one kiss from my clay cold lips
Your time will not be long.

'Down in yonder garden green
Where you and I would walk
The fairest flower that blossoms there
Is withered to the stalk.

'The stalk is withered dry, sweetheart,
So must our love decay
So rest yourself content my dear
Till death calls you away.'

Now have I mourned all on his grave
For a twelve month and a day
I'll set my sails before the wind
To waft me far away.

Folk wisdom knew the value of talking with the departed in order to let go and face the future. Modern psychological research on loss and bereavement also tells us that between nine months and a year is the 'healthy' period for active mourning, and that if uncompleted in this time it can take on morbid and neurotic forms. The song is surely telling us this very clearly.

Lily hugged me and thanked me and we all knew the comfort of witnessing to our common human fragility, and hearing this translated into a song of timeless beauty.

Chapter 8

With my new social work qualification, I now got a job at the Community Drug Project in Camberwell. I wanted to work with younger people and broadly in the 'mental health' area, and the fact that it was based in a Day Centre meant it would be better for me, as my slowly dwindling sight made it stressful to travel around visiting people.

The project was based in Wren Road, in a somewhat scruffy building with bare floorboards and second-hand furniture, in spite of which I felt at home there. I arrived for work on a grey August morning with Wren Road looking like something out of a Dickensian novel. I was taken into the main 'living' area and introduced to Tony Bickersteth, the social work assistant, and some of the regular attenders. I will disguise their names and 'redistribute' some of their stories so that none will be identifiable, though all the events I describe are true. Some of the people are still alive, some holding down responsible jobs, while others, sadly, have died, or I have heard nothing of them for years.

In the first few days I met clients such as Leo, an intense man who could engross you in conversations about poetry and the meaning of life; Glenda, attractive and funny, but given to sudden rages and suicide attempts; Gary, wild and frequently out of control; and Rick, whose cold violence frightened me. Before this I had had very little direct exposure to violence. I remembered from my childhood rages that anger and frustration were as much physical as psychological, but when people are under the influence of certain drugs, such as barbiturates or alcohol, there is no chance of redirecting this energy: so real harm was a constant threat.

Bobby, a beautiful Dubliner, was in the business of 'self-medicating' for a profound, chronic depression. This turned out to be the case with many of the attenders. Using heroin or amphetamine substances, they could capture a sense of wellbeing hardly ever experienced when 'normal'. With the much more lethal barbiturates they could make a bid for temporary oblivion, though it was Russian roulette: the oblivion was not always temporary.

Ben was a charmer: articulate, good looking and flamboyantly dressed with the shoplifted pickings of a trendy Knightsbridge store, he epitomized a certain style of junkie. He and Bob Searchfield, a staff member, regaled me with the story of how Prince Philip had visited earlier in the year. Ben had been dressed to kill for the occasion and, with his persuasive manner and presence, had clearly been marked out by the Prince as a member of staff. On shaking hands with him Ben had remarked, looking pointedly at the sling in which the Prince's left arm was enfolded, 'Had a dirty fix, Sir?'

I was amazed to find how much humour there was in that place. There was despair, cruelty, depression, apathy, viciousness and greed in plenty, but warmth, wit and humour made it bearable, even enjoyable, to work there.

Jim had a pale, sensitive face with beautiful, dark, haunted eyes. He was a committed anarchist and had been one of the Glasgow Eskimos who went up the Clyde in canoes to stop the first nuclear submarine. He was also a lover of art and classical music. He and I became kindred spirits, once his chronic mistrust had melted. One day when we had visited an art gallery and I was frantically rushing off for a meeting, Jim said, 'Frankie, I may be compulsively irresponsible, but you're compulsively responsible. It would be good if we could rub off a bit on each other' – a remark which made a great impact on me.

From this distance it seems bizarre that I once lived for eight hours a day or more in a world where despair, suicide and violence were normal aspects of daily life. It is not easy work. I don't know how 'well' I did it, but it taught me a great deal about myself and about those people who live on the margins.

I learnt to survive being disliked and even hated. In the 'honeymoon' period of the first few months I enjoyed the challenge and mostly liked the attenders. I found no difficulty in listening and in good, classic social-work fashion, empathized with their personal and existential doubts and despairs. I had sailed naïvely in, full of my natural optimism, and this can be infectious. Even some of the most hardbitten addicts seemed to find my presence, initially, a 'shot in the arm', and I use the metaphor intentionally. I remember several remarks on the lines of 'Frankie'll never get on drugs. She doesn't need them. She's high on life.'

With the new injection of hope, which for the moment I represented, there was a lot more talk about coming off drugs or at least stabilizing doses and finding more meaningful ways to make life worth living. But then I became an easy target for their disappointment and disillusion when people found themselves back on the treadmill of homeless hostels and sleeping rough, re-negotiating their 'script' (the prescription from the psychiatrist or the Drug Dependency Unit, picked up daily from the special chemists) and re-establishing their contacts for illegal supplies. Now I was verbally attacked (though, luckily, never physically) or treated with icy indifference. I started to dread going up the road to the Centre, especially if it was my turn to unlock the front door. If I was 30 seconds late, this would be treated as proof that I had no concern for their welfare. They were hurt and angry. I was hurt and angry.

I found myself behaving in loud and confrontational ways, and although I wouldn't recommend that, it was how I showed myself to be human and vulnerable. Out of the ashes of our shouting matches and mutual accusations, for some a phoenix of genuine trust eventually began to emerge. There were dangers in the volatile way I reacted, but if I had hidden behind a too-controlled professionalism, that human contact point might never have been reached.

Emptiness and chaos were things I learnt to look at through some of their haunted, frightened eyes. Roger was in his fifties, scrawny, with a sunken, hunted face and scraggy, greying hair. He had come off drugs in prison and asked if he could go into hospital to help him stay detoxified. On the day of his release, I took him to Greenwich Hospital. I'll never forget the experience of sitting with him in the waiting room. For a fleeting moment I glimpsed utter emptiness stretching before me as far as the eye could see. Time stretching meaninglessly away for ever. Nothing. I wasn't surprised when I heard that Roger had left the hospital and was asking for his script again. It was around this time that I came to realize a less obvious attraction of the drug scene: part of its appeal was that it structured the day for people. There was something to get up for each morning and somewhere to go. Statistics show that depression and suicide often result from chronic unemployment. That moment with Roger taught me what the total loss or lack of structure must be like: through him, I had seen into the void.

I learnt that I could not dodge authority and responsibility for the choices I had made. I became used to being told 'Social workers are just policemen in soft disguise' or 'You're just as bad as doctors or screws, telling us what we can and what we can't do'. I had to recognize that I had power because I was a worker, and I had to enforce that power.

I faced the ultimate accusation one freezing winter's evening when a desperate, underclad and stoned client I was fond of screamed as I locked him out 'If I'm found frozen dead on Camberwell Green in the morning, it'll be all your fault!' Given that this was a real possibility, I found myself face to face with the clearest and most fearful consequence of his and my choices. For one painful minute, I became the agent for yet another, possibly fatal, abandonment.

Nevertheless, it became evident to me that our honesty and clarity on this basic point made it possible to forge more real relationships than if we had dodged the authority issue. Once it is faced and acknowledged (if not necessarily accepted by the client) then you are freed to find a much more equal relationship.

I still have a deep affection for many of those I got to know at the Community Drug Project between 1970 and 1974. I remember teasing Rex, an ex-jazz and rock drummer, who was over six feet tall but had a chronic stoop, his pathetic victim posture. In keeping with his helplessness, one afternoon Rex asked me to make him a cup of tea, because he didn't know how to do it.

'Well, now's the time to learn,' I said.

'Now, Frankie, if you cared about me you'd show it by making me a tea. I've just come in from the freezing cold . . .'

'On the contrary, it shows how much more caring and concerned I am to help you learn the erudite art of tea-making, so you can look after yourself at least in this one way in the future!'

Rex must have been in his early thirties that winter's afternoon in 1971 when he at last learnt how to make a cup of tea.

They all went in and out of detox and rehab like yoyos. High levels of anxiety and depression, together with fears of being overwhelmed by the feelings that the drugs had been used to stave off, often proved too much. We would get a phone call from a hospital or centre, telling us to look out for so-and-so, who had left with no warning. This meant they would be up at Piccadilly scoring until they could persuade their clinic doctor to prescribe for them again.

We always tried to rescue what we could from these episodes. It would have made little sense to harangue them for yet another failure, and we encouraged them to learn from their mistakes. Most of them were in their thirties and forties; some had been on the junk scene for ten years or more and all their friends and peers were on the same scene. It wasn't easy for them to contemplate starting all over again.

It was through the beautiful, haunted eyes of Jim that I saw into the vortex. We became very close and I really understood what he was experiencing when he felt a total sense of despair and chaos at the core of things. Most of us manage to deny the madness we know to be inside us and in the world. Jim's tragedy was that he saw very little else. Eventually he gave up the struggle and allowed the drugs and his lifestyle to take their fatal toll.

His funeral was one of the most moving events I have experienced. He had no relatives that he knew of. Fellow junkies and workers contributed to his coffin and burial so that it could be done 'properly', rather than handing over his body to the local authority. One of his friends asked us all to contribute a poem or reading or, in my case, a song. It was a tribute to how this sad man affected us all that such a funeral took place.

> Mourn not the dead that in the dark earth lie,
> Dust unto dust,
> The calm, sweet earth that mothers all who die,
> As all men must.

I set this anarchist poem from earlier in the century to a powerful, keening tune, to sing at the graveside. It can still move me to tears. Not I, not anyone could ultimately help Jim through his dark night of the soul. Several years later I had a vivid dream of Jim smiling with such knowing and such peace, I could only feel glad for him.

Jim, amongst others, taught me my limitations. It's all too easy when faced with intelligent, attractive people of one's own age, playing Russian roulette, to feel one will do everything within one's power and ability to try and 'save' them from an early death. This can lead to a feeling of resentment towards the clients who for the most part don't respond as one would wish, and eventually, to burn-out. It soon became clear to me that I could not lead their lives for them, but had to make them take responsibility for their choices.

Paradoxically, one of the outcomes of the compassionate British response to addiction – the setting up of the Drug Dependency Units in 1968 – was to turn addicts into medical patients. I often heard the defence 'I'm sick, I simply can't help it!' and the corollary of this was abnegation of the choice to stay on drugs or come off them. I considered I had done a good job if I heard one of them admit a *reason* for being on drugs. If someone could say 'I choose', then there was at least some hope. Of course they might also say 'I choose to end my life.' Sad as it might be, that too was a choice and I wouldn't argue with someone's right to make it.

All the time I was at the CDP I continued singing, and as time went on, I began to recognize that my working life connected in a new way with the kind of human experience that I was constantly singing about. I gradually came to feel that, having been exposed to a deeper, darker pool of human imagination and emotions, my singing was becoming more integrated with who I was and what I saw around me. Far from having moved away from my base as a singer, I had found a place from which I could truly begin to own the material of the songs. Being involved in the things that were happening about people, between people, kept me emotionally fed in a way that I could use and plough back into the songs.

I became a lot more selective in what I chose to sing and why. I began to look at ballads like 'Lady Diamond' or 'Barbara Allen' with fresh eyes, becoming more aware that the events in those songs were still going on: people *did* get murdered out of jealousy; people *were* still oppressed for trying to break out of old systems and ways of thought; people *were* still dying because of the loss of love in their lives.

Both as a social worker and as a singer I had to avoid becoming so swamped by a song, or by a situation, that I couldn't function properly. I learnt, in both areas of my life, to be open and able to bring the whole of myself, yet keep that little, crucial distance which keeps the channel of communication clear. As a person, as a social worker and as a singer I was becoming more of a piece. Maybe this was the beginning of the process out of which the voice workshops grew.

Chapter 9

I was still a member of the Critics Group and our various projects and researches continued, but tensions between Ewan and members of the group were beginning to mount. Ewan's incapacity to brook criticism became increasingly evident and those members who would voice criticisms on behalf of the group would often be verbally annihilated by his articulate, mind-blitzing self-defence. He could always produce half a dozen authorities to justify any action he took. One year, Brian and I had been chosen spokespersons for most of the group's discontent, and faced the full power of his vitriol.

Then, after a particularly successful Festival of Fools, Ewan collapsed with a severe illness. When he had recovered enough he gathered us together in Beckenham and, unaccountably, offered us the opportunity to direct ourselves. But we became anxious about 'getting it right' in his eyes, and this colluded with the anxiety he must have felt in backing off and letting us flounder by ourselves.

Brian and I were under immense pressure, combining work and the Critics Group, and we could feel stresses in the group rising. Predicting an almighty bust-up, we took a painful decision and left. The following winter the bust-up happened and the eight years of the Critics Group came to a bitter end. It was a sad finale which many people took years to get over. Some of the group never saw Ewan again, but some were generous enough to come and be part of his memorial weekend a year after he died in October 1989.

Our decision to leave the group had not been an easy one. Brian had admired and respected Ewan for years before the Critics Group was formed – though he saw Ewan's faults and foibles more clearly than most of us, he was also the one most able to accept them. But after leaving it soon became clear to us that we had stayed too long. Undoubtedly, Ewan was a genius with an immense amount to offer and I had learnt a lot from Peggy, too. But two or three years is the longest one should sit at the feet of such a contradictory man.

I only began to be fully 'my own singer' when I left the Critics Group, and this was the start of that subtlest of processes, the process of truly finding one's own voice. A year or so after our break with the group, at the end of a concert in Brighton when I had sung 'Barbara Allen', Brian remarked, 'You found it tonight, Frankie. You and the ballad were monumental. You were simply *there*.'

At last I felt ready. Tonic Records had offered me the chance of doing a solo album back in 1967. I had been thrilled, but something inside had told me I wasn't yet ready to take on a whole LP. Now I felt I could handle the 'big' ballads as well as more lyrical and light-hearted songs.

So in 1971 I gave birth to *Lovely on the Water*, my first solo LP. The title track was a song collected by Vaughan Williams. I haven't sung it for several years, but I remember the last verse clearly:

Now Tower Hill is crowded
With women weeping sore
For their husbands, sons and sweethearts
Gone to fight the cruel war.

In the early 1970s Topic was an influential but very small concern: the 'studio' we used was a large, wood-panelled room in Hampstead with curtains hung over the windows and doors to keep out extraneous noise. In spite of these, jet planes coming over meant that we had to stop and start on several songs. We made the entire record in one day. Though there are some tracks I now cringe at, the singing has fire and spirit – ultimately more important than technical perfection. The reviews my LP got in those heady days at the height of the folk revival were extensive and, to my great delight, very positive.

By now Brian and I had moved to a flat in Stockwell, South London. Brian had begun reading Jung, who became a rôle model to us in one area of his life: while happily married to Emma, he had publicly had a lengthy, open relationship with his pupil, Toni Wolff. At this point Brian was seriously involved with a fellow student, Irene. Although, inevitably, I felt threatened, it felt much more important that Brian and I were honest with each other. I met and liked Irene and came to recognize that it was how I felt about myself, rather than any jealousy I might feel about her, that determined whether I could feel secure and happy. Brian and I talked a lot and decided that neither of us felt we could promise to be monogamous. But we did make a strong commitment to mutual trust, promising that we would tell each other if we fell for, or even had a fling with, someone else.

In the spring of 1971 I had another serious crisis about my sight. By now I had very little vision in the left eye. What reading I could manage was done with my right eye with the aid of a thick magnifying glass. The glaucoma in my left had been difficult to stabilize and for years I had been on drops and tablets to reduce the build-up of fluid. My consultant decided to try a treatment for the pressure called cyclocryothermy – a freezing and unfreezing of the eye which could reduce the pressure without the dangers inherent in surgery. I went into Moorfields for a few days and the procedure seemed successful, so they took me off all the medication for glaucoma.

I was discharged on the Friday and went with Brian to spend a weekend with my parents at Hoddesdon. Before lunch on Saturday we went for a walk to a little country pub half a mile away. On the way we passed some glorious pale pink almond blossom, like candyfloss, against a clear blue spring sky. As we talked and drank outside the Woodman's Arms I noticed a slight blurring of my sight, but I put it down to the brightness of the mid-day sun. However, on the way back I was frightened to discover that I could barely see the blossom which had so arrested me just an hour before. We had lunch hoping it would clear up, but it didn't, so I phoned Moorfields. They told me to get up to them as soon as possible.

It was a frightening journey. Though I was used to carrying a white cane to cross streets and on the underground, this Saturday afternoon was the first time I needed someone's elbow to guide me. It felt strange and scary. By the time we got to City Road I could see very little. They examined me and found that I now had glaucoma in the right eye. It is possible that I had had it for years and that the systemic treatment for the left eye had been keeping the right under control. With the cessation of that treatment, the condition in the right eye had worsened rapidly. I was given massive injections of diuretics and in a matter of hours the sight had improved, but not enough for me to be able to read an ordinary print book magazine or newspaper ever again.

Later in the year my father was made redundant. He was 55 years old. On the Friday evening, at the firm's annual dinner dance, he was presented with a gold watch for 25 years' service. The following Tuesday he was asked into the managing director's office and told that his job, along with scores of others, had 'disappeared'.

It took a few days for him to get over the shock and numbness, but within a week my parents had put their house in Hoddesdon on the market and at the first opportunity they went house-hunting in the Lake District. Within a month or two they had bought Hill Crest, a two-bedroomed bungalow just off the road from Kendal to Windermere. They were surrounded with fields, with a front view over the distant Kentmere hills.

Dad showed characteristic unwillingness to bow down under the rod, suggesting to the firm that he would be a useful trouble-shooter for firms in the north of England and in Scotland to which the Rolling Mills sent materials. Within months of becoming 'redundant' he was back to working part-time as a peripatetic consultant. For Mum the whole event was a blessed relief. Away from the stresses of being a manager but in sympathy with the floor workers (perhaps a reason why he was sacked) Dad became more relaxed and talkative. My parents loved being back in the Lakes and going for regular walks in the Fells, and their new home became a much-loved haven for me over the next eleven years.

Life at CDP went on in its unpredictable way. For a time we tried to channel the energy of the attenders away from drugs by running art, jewellery-making or drama groups. It was a pretty thankless effort.

With such difficult and unrewarding work, we came to feel that it was essential to have our batteries recharged on a regular basis. Fortunately for us, the need for this kind of support for people working in such demanding fields as homelessness, addiction and recidivism was becoming widely recognized, and the South London Consortium was set up, directed by an ex-monk called Guy Braithwaite. The Consortium was made up of day centres, night shelters, counselling and advice organizations, rehabilitation hostels and hostels for the single homeless. There were seminar courses, talks and subcommittees to set up coordinating groups with local and central government.

By 1971 a number of us in the Consortium had set up the CTS (Co-operative Training Services) courses, and I discovered my fascination with training. I began using rôle play and simulation for my chunk of the Orientation Courses and learnt how valuable it was to get students exploring through experience rather than discussion alone.

Again and again social workers on the courses talked about what they felt was expected of them and what they felt was correct 'professional' behaviour. But this was often clearly at odds with what they were actually feeling. Setting up rôle plays revealed how much better we were at 'playing' the clients than being authentically ourselves. As our real clients could always pick up on any discrepancy between what we were saying and what we were really thinking and feeling, this discrepancy provided them with an ideal springboard for the game-playing and manipulation which so distresses and undermines workers. It became clear that we were setting ourselves up for this to happen and would continue to do so unless we found a way of being more authentic. It was a constant challenge for us to find ways of being honest which were not judgemental or rejecting and collusive, and that gave useful, respectful feedback.

I also explored Co-Counselling. Guy introduced some of us to John Southgate, a group worker who was interested in setting up a network of counsellors on the broad Left. Some of us got very excited about this, seeing the necessity to close the gap between the two paradigms – the political and the psychological – and becoming aware of the idea that 'the personal is political' which was filtering through from the Women's Movement.

So John arranged for a Sri Lankan woman called Savitri to run some training weekends, largely on the Co-Counselling model. I was amazed at some of the results, especially by two personal insights I gained.

On the first occasion the group were given an exercise requiring us to create a little dramatized version of ourselves at our most put-upon. I ran around like the proverbial chicken without its head: 'I simply must get off to this important meeting and drat! there's the phone – a friend needing my support – and I've got the annual report to write and I need to arrange for a client to get down to Andover and the National Abortion Campaign want me to sing at the rally and I want to write a song for it and how can I possibly be expected to do all this and lose my sight at the same time?!'

It was very funny but also very telling. Who *expected* me to do all this? When it dawned on me that we impose many of these demands on ourselves, it was oh so easy to see and oh so difficult to do anything about it. It took me a long time to admit that it was a sense of self-importance as well as my genuine commitment to social justice that had me driving myself so hard.

The other insight came when we were all paired off for a mini Co-Counselling session. I was with a woman I didn't particularly like, finding her a little 'heady' and somewhat lacking in warmth. During that half of the time when it was my turn to talk and hers to listen, intervening to follow up any statements I made that seemed to affect me strongly, she said 'What happens if you say "I'm afraid of going blind"?'

I said it and broke down in great waves of sobbing. She allowed this and suggested periodically that I repeat the statement. She was excellent. That morning I wept out fears that I had never allowed myself to feel.

Eventually I was able to say 'I'm afraid of going blind' to the whole group, meaning it and not being swamped by it. It was now acknowledged as a fact and I could face it as such. This brought tremendous relief and released more energy than usual, even for me.

I now had to ask for help when I wanted to cross a busy road or get information from train indicators. I began to wonder how my future, especially my work, would be affected as this deterioration continued. The cataracts were thickening as well as irreversible damage being done by the barely controlled glaucoma, but all the doctors I saw at Moorfields agreed that I needed to wait before contemplating the cataract removal. 'There are too many risks involved, so while you've got the sight you have and while you're managing . . .'

And then I was told about Archie Lineburger, a blind group therapist in Philadelphia. He was black, played an excellent jazz saxophone, and was reputed to be an excellent therapist. He had been told about me too, and had offered to have me sit in on his groups if I were ever visiting.

Until that moment I had somehow ruled out the possibility of running groups, but here was a totally blind group therapist – and in the field of drug addiction to boot! My head started buzzing. I couldn't raise the money for a trip to the States, but if there was work to help with the expenses . . . Brian and I were only weeks away from a holiday in Canada, but I was also to sing at the Mariposa Festival and at Fiddlers Green, the Toronto folk club.

We went to Canada as planned, and at the Festival I met Kenny Goldstein, then head of the Folklore Department at the University of Pennsylvania, who asked me if I could come to the Philadelphia Folk Festival one year. They couldn't pay my fare from the UK, but they would pay me a reasonable fee if I could manage to get there. At Fiddlers Green I met Debbie Pheasant. She too worked with addicts and – coincidence of coincidences – lived in the same house as Archie Lineburger. We exchanged addresses and promised to write. The pull towards Philly was getting stronger and I decided that I would try to get over somehow the very next year, both for the Festival and to spend some time with Archie Lineburger.

At the suggestion of Bob Searchfield (the CDP Director) and Martin (the Chairperson) I applied to the Ford Foundation for funding. To my amazement they gave me $2,000 by way of a Travel Study Award.

I arranged to set off early in August 1973, starting with the Philadelphia Folk Festival and then spend two months visiting Drug Projects around the country. Part of me was pretty scared about going off and travelling on my own for what seemed, then, like a long time. At that time, I think I could see about as much as I can now, but because I'm comparing it with how little I saw a few months back, it feels like a lot of sight. Then, because of the recent deterioration and the knowledge that it was inevitably going to get worse, my awareness was coloured by a degree of fear and apprehension. I devoured what I could still see with great intensity and with an even more intense awareness because I knew how fragile I was.

America

Chapter 10

My first port of call in the States was New York, where I stayed for two days before going down to Philadelphia. Paula Ballan was arranging all the artists' contracts and she had invited me to stay with her on my arrival. It turned out that she worked with drug addicts, too.

With Paula I visited Staten Island, Manhattan, the Statue of Liberty, and saw so many cultures represented by cafés, shops, places of worship, styles of dress. I drank it all in. After two days Paula had to rush off and I took my first independent step on American soil. In my blue jeans and red shirt, I strode out in search of a cab. It was a quiet Sunday morning with a cloudless sky. Whenever I find myself on my own somewhere totally new, I remember that morning and the excited anticipation of new adventure.

Half an hour later I embarked on the first of many Greyhound journeys. Debbie Pheasant met me at the other end and as we trained out from the centre of Philadelphia to her home in Germantown, she explained a trifle warily that she lived in a house with four others, three of whom were 'married' to each other. She was clearly relieved that I found nothing strange or amiss in this relationship. Archie was 'married' both to Rava, his girlfriend from university days, and Alice, a blind woman he had met when they were both being trained to use their Seeing Eye dogs. The fourth person was John, Rava's brother. Rava and John made puppets and gave puppet shows. Alice was a social worker with the visually handicapped, and played piano; Rava also sculpted and Archie was a saxophonist. They were a stimulating household.

After I had settled into my room Debbie said 'I hope you're not too tired – I've arranged for us to go out for a meal this evening with Ethel Raim and her husband. She's really keen to meet you.'

My cup was overflowing.

Ethel was a folklorist and collector as well as a singer, and had started running weekly Vocal Workshops in Philly and in New York to teach the Balkan singing style and songs. We adored each other from that first meeting. We explored our musical tastes, our ideas and political understandings, and with Ethel my awareness and anger about the way women were treated began to grow.

In the following weeks I wrote several songs which marked a watershed in my development. One was called 'Who Are You Fighting, Brother?'. One verse ends:

> But I've seen all the love that you keep deep inside,
> So now you treat me like an enemy.

Another verse is:

> You've fought well and hard, my brother,
> But there's one fight you still must win –
> Learn when to be weak and when to give in
> And so come to see the real enemy.

I wrote this song for an extraordinary man named Brian MacDonald.

As Philly is the largest and one of the most prestigious of the folk festivals, I got invitations from organizers of folk clubs, coffee houses and other festivals to appear at their establishments. I was able to consider them by arranging to visit local drug agencies at the same time, and this was how I managed to set up a trip that took me to up-state New York, Massachusetts, Arizona, San Francisco, Los Angeles and then back to New York and Long Island.

I spent two weeks sitting in on Archie's groups and taking part in general community meetings. I found both the place and Archie very impressive, and became convinced that blindness was no obstacle to being a group worker, though I realized I would need a good deal more experience to be anything like as skilled as Archie was. Then I decided to stay on in Philadelphia and take in other agencies, including the section of the Probation service that dealt with drug offenders. I found it headed by a man younger than myself with one of the most 'lived-in' faces I've ever seen. This was Brian MacDonald.

Brian was immensely attractive and we had one of those odd chemical reactions to each other. But, as with Alasdair Clayre, there was a strong attraction and a last-minute pull away from sexual involvement. Over the months I stayed in the States I spent a great deal of time with Brian – one of the most extraordinary people I have ever known. He had been involved with the Berrigan Brothers (the radical Catholic priests) in what was known as 'the Media break-in'. They had managed to get into the FBI and find the files on all the anti-war activists in the area, much of the 'information' consisting of provable fabrications. His wife Alice had been a prominent black activist and had been murdered in the street by muggers several years before. When the US had started bombing Cambodia, Brian had chained himself to the White House railings and gone on hunger strike for over 30 days. He knew Shirley Maclaine, Buffy Sainte Marie and, most unlikely of all, Henry Kissinger with whom he had a strange love-hate relationship, loathing his political beliefs and yet feeling drawn to the sheer energy and personal charm of the man.

When I left Philly for New York, Brian came with me. He was from a well-to-do Irish American family and was not averse to a little luxury, for all his radical politics. It was Labour Day weekend and he insisted that we stay at the splendid, wood-panelled Algonquin Hotel, of Dorothy Parker fame, where we drank $24 bottles of Châteauneuf-du-Pape (1983 prices!). I had never experienced such indulgence.

Brian was a courageous political activist with a burning desire to see injustices lessened, yet he had some pretty classic male ways of defending himself emotionally. When I wrote 'Who Are You Fighting, Brother?' I wondered if the song was too personal to speak to other people, so I tried it out on women friends. Their responses told me that it could resonate more widely, which it has done over the years, even with women whose male partners are downright conservative.

During that time, I heard of the killing of President Allende, and the murder of the Chilean writer and singer Victor Jara. As a prisoner with thousands of others in the Santiago stadium, he had sung and played until the guards took his guitar away, breaking all his fingers and killing him two days later. This was a powerful reminder of the power of song, so intolerable to tyrannical powers when they come up against it.

By the time I returned to New York Ethel had started her Balkan singing classes, which I was eager to attend. We had arranged for me to take part in one on a Wednesday evening in Greenwich Village.

'The village' was just as I had pictured it: little Lebanese cafés, Italian coffee shops, Bohemian boutiques, bookshops galore and chess players in Washington Square.

About twelve of us took part in Ethel's all-woman class. Ethel introduced me to the group and began with her warm-up exercises. 'Hey!' she called, smiling. We all called 'Hey!' back. Higher and lower and even higher, when the sound became 'Ee'. We slid up and down and found a deliciously relaxing sound at the bottom of our range. I remembered doing it as a child, lying in my bed croaking gently like a contented frog. 'Making that sound really helps to relax the throat and jaw,' Ethel said.

We held notes for as long as we could and then she asked us to go round the circle, each one sustaining a 'Hey'. For all my experience and the fact that only weeks before I'd sung to a crowd of 20,000 at the Philly Festival, when it came to my turn I could feel the anxiety rise. Something that sounded horribly squeaky emerged from my mouth. It's a memory I've often recounted to reassure people in my workshops that I know just what that feels like.

I was freer the second time round, then I got into the sheer joy of the group singing. Ethel taught us a three-part

Yugoslav song. With our voices opened and strengthened from the warm-up, we sounded pretty good by the end of the evening.

We didn't only sound good – we felt good. We all looked different at the end. I could see enough to tell that faces had softened and especially that we were all sitting and standing in a more relaxed manner as well as more upright. Our speaking voices, too, were fuller and richer.

I guess it was the singer in me that revelled in the sounds we made and songs we learnt, while the social worker in me observed with delight the changes that came over individuals in the group. As a group, too, we quickly developed a sense of support and collective identity. Though I had no idea at the time, this was the experience that would eventually change the direction of my life.

I visited numerous drug projects up and down the country, including a unique one at Phoenix, Arizona, which combined a free clinic with a 24-hour ambulance and emergency service. In the States the reasons for the drug epidemic were clear enough to see: phenomenal amounts of money to be made at the top and, at the bottom, the alienation of unemployed youth, many of them fearing to be caught up in a long, savage war overseas. Yet the quality of the response to youth in crisis left Britain way behind. The British way of dealing with the issue was an establishment one, run by respectable consultants. In the States many of the workers were radicalized Vietnam war veterans, ex-prisoners and ex-junkies, working alongside university graduates, para-medical staff and nurses wearing jeans and T-shirts. I found a flexibility and a vitality noticeable by their absence in Britain.

From Phoenix I went on by Greyhound bus across the desert to California. Friends in Phoenix had warned me 'It's such a long, dreary trip – all that endless desert!' But as I sat near the back of the bus, peering out through my monocular, I saw a magical landscape. The colours and shapes changed endlessly.

As the sun moved round to the west, the weird outlines of huge rock formations stood out against a paling sky. Cactus trees, like strange beings in a myriad of dramatic postures, watched us as we slid past them.

I spent a week in Los Angeles visiting prisons, detox centres, rehab houses, employment training centres and street agencies, escorted around by a worker called Eduardo. He was large, dark-skinned, tough and one of the most 'found' men I have encountered. He had spent 14 years in San Quentin. Prison does terrible things to people, but on rare occasions people create miracles out of their experience and Eduardo was one such. He was so articulate, he could run rings round starchy hospital administrators and addicts alike. My respect and affection for him grew daily. He would take me back to my hotel room at all hours of the day and night, envelop me in a gentle bear hug, kiss me on the forehead and leave. I felt utterly safe with him.

After LA, my trail continued on up Highway 101 through Central Valley to San Francisco, where I stayed with Roger and Carol Smith. (Roger was a founder of the famous Haight-Ashbury Free Clinic.) The address was 'Paradise Drive', and I could see why when I looked out on my first morning there with my monocular at the blue, blue bay and the reddish glow of the Golden Gate suspension bridge. Palm and eucalyptus trees grew around the house. Roger was co-owner of a sailing boat with the sign of a dove of peace painted on its large white sail. We went out sailing on the bay, laughing and singing as the spray saturated us. We rode the painted, bell-ringing trams and talked drugs, sex, politics and therapy.

I was invited to sing at the Freight and Salvage coffee house, the best known folk club in Berkeley. I began to sing with Holly Tannen, a dulcimer player and singer, and with Susie Rothfield, then only 19 but already a fine singer, guitar player and fiddler. Holly arranged for the three of us to do some singing back in LA.

Then came an episode that quite suddenly and unexpectedly challenged me on a subject I felt and still feel very strongly about. I was booked for a festival at Nassau, Long

Island, to do a presentation on women in traditional British song. This workshop had a major effect on my sense of myself as a woman and of our history, already heightened by my contact with Ethel some three weeks before.

The very next day, I was part of a workshop on amorous and erotic songs. I was happy to be part of it, even as the only woman with three men, being familiar with the pre-industrial repertoire and its songs that show women to be as lusty as men and just as frequently initiators of sexual encounters. A few lines will illustrate my point:

Oh my handsome, fair young man, you're tired of your
work,
... For mowing is hard labour and weakening to the back.
Yes, mowing is hard labour and it you must forsake
But around my little meadow you may use your fork and
rake.

I said my pretty fair young maid, pray do not on me frown
For if I stayed the summer long I could not mow it down,
For it is such a pleasant place, it grows such crops of grass
It is well watered by the spring that makes it grow so fast.

I had a number of tender, humorous or joyously defiant songs to sing for the workshop and was horrified when one very well known participant proceeded to sing songs that were blatantly and horribly pornographic. They were everything I hate about the genre: they objectified women, were written from a totally male perspective, and were crude and gross, lacking in any poetry, tenderness or mutuality.

An awful dilemma arises when you find yourself on stage with someone who is doing something you find profoundly obscene and upsetting. I made the choice to say that I found these songs unsettling and demeaning and I needed to make that public.

As a consequence, I was accused of having no sense of humour, of being touchy and 'taking things personally'.

'How true!' I said.

Happily, some women in the audience backed me up publicly and a large number came up later to say how grateful they were that I'd been willing to put myself on the line. In an ironic way I can be grateful to the chauvinism and insensitivity of that man, because it was so extreme that it gave me a clear opportunity to make my feelings known. It can be much more difficult, I've found, when the songs are of a less obviously offensive type, yet still subtly put women down. The future was to produce many public dilemmas and dissents, not all of them predictable, arising out of the never-ending debate around sexual politics.

Throughout the first trip to the States, I phoned Brian each week. Though always delighted to speak to each other, we were both growing as a result of the separation. It was a good feeling and an important realization for me: that I didn't have to feel that I was rejecting him in order to feel also that I wanted more time to explore on my own, to develop the confidence that I could feel growing inside me.

My return to London was a week away. My good friends Ernie and Jeri Drucker had invited me to spend time with them in New York. The eccentric Peter Johnson had invited me to do concerts in the Boston area. The Washington Folklore Society had invited me. I knew there was work for me back in California if I wanted it. Also my love affair with the Bay had been augmented by a delicious love affair with Joe, Roger's partner in ownership of the boat. I had every incentive to commit the first irresponsible act of my life. I wrote a letter to Martin Mitcheson, chair of the CDP management committee, saying that I was going to extend my unpaid leave for another two months!

I never regretted my decision. On my trips up and down the East Coast I began to feel that Jeri and Ernie's apartment was my second home. I grew to love them and their area. Fall was underway and we would walk by the river watching the leaves change and the children playing baseball. I learnt to find my way round the subways of New York and found a way of making myself 'neutral' so that I felt as safe as I could, given the number of drunks and stoned and generally crazy people that city generates. For the most part I found that if I treated people with trust they treated me likewise.

Through my time in the States my confidence on stage grew in leaps and bounds. Most of my singing in the UK had up till then been in folk clubs and festivals, which meant that I rarely did more than two half-hour sets. This may sound like a lot of singing (especially for an unaccompanied singer), but in the folk concerts and coffee houses of the States it was quite common for the performer to take the entire evening, which could mean as much as two hours of solid singing. Occasionally I was required to do two separate concerts in one evening – maybe as much as two and a half hours of nonstop singing with only small intermissions.

What I learnt to do over these months was to create my programme so as to thread songs together with either historic, thematic or imagistic connections, so as to make the set a whole. This was partially borne of the fact that I couldn't see enough to glance at a set list and know what came next.

This turned out to be a great blessing. I never do the same programme the identical way twice. I may do largely the same material for a while, but moving the songs around in relation to each other means that I can always find new meanings in the way they are juxtaposed.

As the trip came to an end, I went on getting invitations to return, including a tempting one from a woman who was to head up the all-women caucus at the National Drug Conference in Chicago the following March. She asked if I would participate as a drugs worker and a singer of women's songs. But I could make no promises before going back to London and consulting Brian and CDP. After many sad farewells I found myself in a taxi, driving through snow towards the airport.

Goodbye, New York. Goodbye, the United States of America – land of contradictions, of extremes, the loathsome and the lovable. I grew some large new part of myself while on your strange shores.

Chapter 11

It was a treat to see family and friends again. However, it didn't banish from my thoughts the tempting invitations that called me back to the States. I talked at great length to Brian and then to colleagues and management at CDP, and eventually decided that I would go back to the US after working two months' notice, which would give them time to replace me, and me time to hand over.

I accepted the first engagement I had been offered, which meant returning in early March. We planned that Brian would come out in late May for his five weeks' holiday. After that, according to how we both felt, we would make decisions about where we might eventually live.

Before going back I spent some time with Mum and Dad up in their new bungalow. We walked the hills and as ever Mum and I found anything and everything to talk about. I loved their little home, especially the patio outside the door, sheltered from the road with a view across fields in which sheep and cows and clumps of trees clustered like filigree fortresses up on the skyline. I had sent weekly tapes from the States about my doings, a habit that persists to this day. Mum, likewise, sends me a weekly cassette, addressing it to the appropriate time and place so that with luck it will catch me on my wanderings.

I felt very sad leaving everyone again so soon. I recall sitting on the Icelandic Airline plane feeling disconsolate and wondering if I had done the right thing. I had also become much closer to a certain Paul McKeever during those weeks after my return from the States.

I had interviewed Paul for the job of Senior Social Worker at CDP and had found him intriguing and attractive from the moment I met him. He had dark, Italian/Irish good looks and a working-class background. In spite of scholarships to boarding school, and to read English at Oxford, and a postgraduate degree in social work at Bristol, he held defiantly to his Neasden accent. When interviewing people for CDP I always looked for someone with a creative talent other than the work. Paul's was writing. He had a quality, not uncommon in working-class men, of romanticism disguised by cynicism: in him it had a unique flavour that came out clearly in his writing – mostly stories about rather bleak, squalid lives of drug addicts and delinquent kids. Yet, however stark the stories, they were somehow chastening and uplifting. He had this effect on me, live, as well, so I never tired of his company. A romantic entanglement developed, and somehow Paul, his actress lover Viv, Brian and I managed to stay friends and work out the logistics needed to deal with it.

Brian MacDonald had phoned me in England to say he was going out to San Francisco in February, giving me a friend's phone number where he planned to be staying when I arrived. I phoned the number from New York, to be told he'd never turned up, though some of his trunks had. The friend had no idea where he was. The farm where he used to live outside Philly was now occupied by other people who similarly had no idea where the previous tenants had gone. The whole thing was a mystery. Holly Tannen, with whom I had sung on my last visit, had said I could stay with her any time, but this was not the way I'd expected things to be. The mysterious Brian MacDonald was living up to form again.

Off I went to Boston, back to New York and then on down to Philly. When I reached the Germantown household, something of the Brian MacDonald mystery was solved. There on the kitchen table was a local newspaper with the headline 'Philadelphia Probation Chief on Drugs Charge in Mexico'. It seemed that he had gone off on holiday south of the border with two friends and had finished up in jail on a drugs charge. Later I heard from a mutual friend that the charges had been dismissed when they had come up in court.

Later still, news came that Brian had gone into retreat for a while. With Brian anything was possible. Next news was that he was working in LA. I received a number of messages over the next decade that he was coming to a concert, but he never turned up. Phone numbers he left me never found an answering voice. The full mystery of Brian looks like remaining unsolved for ever.

The drugs conference I was invited to in Chicago was held in a monstrous concrete, glass and steel building known as the Statler Hilton. To spend 48 hours in one of these hideous enclosed environments is to lose touch with nature altogether, but for all this it was a fascinating weekend. The Women's Caucus was full of lively, voluble women waking up to how almost the whole mental health world, including the drug helpers, was male and white and riddled with the unconscious prejudices thereof. I was introduced to the work of authors like Phyllis Chesler, author of *Women and Madness*, which later became a bible in my work.

I had been invited as a singer as well as a drugs worker. Among the songs I sang was 'Doors to my Mind', about one woman's struggle from prostitution and drug abuse to a sense of worth, and of the support and strength gained from other women with similar experiences. She was a composite of many women I had met, especially out in the Bay area. The song was received with rapturous applause, and tears of recognition.

I did go to hear a couple of papers in the main body of the conference, which consisted mostly of men in sober suits talking learnedly of this and that research finding – in marked contrast to the colourful clothes and debates in the women's area. I was both excited and alarmed when the women asked me to sing 'Doors to my Mind' as the entire contribution from our caucus to the plenary session on Sunday afternoon. 'That says everything we want to say and in a way we want to communicate it.'

My knees were shaking as I mounted the platform and opened my mouth. Some of the audience were clearly nonplussed at this unorthodox contribution, but the women's attention and support were so wholehearted that my nerves vanished and I sang my heart out. I felt immensely honoured to be chosen by these women, many of whom had been to hell and back, to be their spokesister. My use of 'sister' and 'sisterhood' probably stems from that weekend when I felt its power directed through me.

From Chicago I flew to San Francisco to stay with Holly. We arranged an extensive tour on which she and Susie Rothfield were to accompany my songs. I had an exquisite trip through the Mojave desert with them, some friends and the lovely Joe – co-owner of the sailing boat on which we had spent those halcyon days the summer before. The desert blooms for just two or three weeks at a different time each year, and we were lucky enough to catch it. The Joshua trees seemed to stretch out friendly limbs covered in trumpet-shaped flowers, the desert floor was bright with pink, yellow and cream cactus flowers and Joe's van smelt like a perfumed garden.

Then it was on, down the coastal road to California. I've a bizarre collection of memories from that journey – oranges growing by the side of a suburban road, apple dolls at the Renaissance fair, the huge response to my singing of Peggy's song 'I'm Gonna Be an Engineer', Bill – our guide – telling us of the adventures of the Tinker of Tomlach, spellbinding us with the doings of the little people and the vitality of the Irish language . . .

One place followed another until I found myself back at Philly for the Spring Festival, during which Brian arrived from London. I remember so clearly my delight on seeing him. Luck was on our side, as Brian had been involved in an industrial dispute of the Addiction Research Unit, which was awaiting arbitration. As this was likely to take more than five weeks, he had come out on an open ticket, leaving a list of addresses all round the States in case his colleagues needed to contact him.

Now Brian and I could share some of the experiences and the people I had talked to him about. He and Archie met and talked sociology and political theory, ten to the dozen. We explored Greenwich Village, where I had sung earlier in the year and been given a magnificent review in the *New York Times*. We went to parties and singsongs and gradually Brian's shyer, more diffident manner lessened.

With Brendan, a friend who had come over from London, and Holly, we flew up to 'mile high city', Denver, marvelling at the Rockies capped with snow, and hired a cart to drive down to the Garden of the Gods, near Colorado Springs.

We travelled on by Greyhound bus to visit friends of Holly's in Taos, New Mexico, who had given up good jobs in academia to build an adobe house amidst the semi-desert, grow a baby daughter and vegetables, keep goats and weave beautiful cloth. The glory of the place, with the smell of sage drifting from the shrub-covered plain and snow glistening on the distant peaks of the Sangre del Christo mountains, was best viewed from the outhouse toilet. I have never enjoyed my bodily functions so much! We visited the Rio Grande and sat naked in the hot springs, tumbling out when it became too scalding into the cold, cold waters of the river.

We spent several weeks around the Bay and I did more concerts and received more enthusiastic reviews. It was considered very exotic to mix ancient, supernatural ballads with modern, feminist songs, expressing my feelings as to where the connections lay.

Then Brian and I, Holly, Susie and some friends went off to the legendary Sweets Mill Music Camp. The site was in the Sierra Foothills – a small lake surrounded by trees and log cabins of various shapes and sizes. Brian and I were allotted the Tree House and slept under the stars.

Camp was attended by 70 to 80 people, the numbers trebling at weekends, all of whom sang, danced, played instruments, spun, wove, dyed or made pots. There was no formal organization: just a blackboard outside the main house where people would announce their workshops or put up requests for a particular class.

In this informal manner, a range of activities went on from dawn to dusk. I remember songs of the sea, songs from the textile industry, ballads, gospel, Carter family songs, country fiddle styles and much more. We swam in the lake, only those in their early teens self-consciously clad in bathing suits. There were children, people in their seventies and all ages between.

We flew back to New York with Holly and Susie for our first New York engagement. I had literally five dollars left. Brian was called back to London and left next morning. He had enjoyed his time in the States, but we had already decided that I would return to London when my engagements were over at the end of September. I had been 'on the road' for five months now and was longing to be back in my own flat. It was then I realized that, gipsy though I am, I do need a base to return to.

At the last festival of the trip I decided to take an enormous risk and sing all 30 verses of 'Tam Lin'. Given that there were some 20,000 people sitting on the grass in front of the main stage, many of them bluegrass fans clutching their beer cans, this was not only brave but foolhardy. Somehow it worked. The crowd quietened as I sunk myself into the mystery of the song, and many were transported by this tale of trans-formation. Susie and Holly joined me afterwards and we ended with the rousing 'I'm Gonna Be an Engineer'.

Two days later, a woman told me that her husband had heard the song and become able at last to understand what happened to women. She had been trying to separate from him and this song had given him the strength to let her go, to find her own independent path. Years later, a completely different man told me that hearing 'Tam Lin' had allowed him to accept the break-up of his marriage and find a place of trust and peace he had never thought possible again.

It's almost frightening to realize the responsibility of carrying these songs. Yet as long as I surrender to the song –

make myself a vehicle for the song and not the song a vehicle for me – then it is not really a 'personal' responsibility. It is, rather, a privilege, but one that carries the need for constant vigilance. I have to respect the songs and keep myself 'clear' so that they can sing through me, so that I don't 'get in the way'. Only then can the songs touch people with the depths of possibility that these stories speak of.

Training and Theatre,
Voice Workshops and Therapy

Chapter 12

I returned to England unsure what direction to take next, so we both signed on at Brixton Labour Exchange. Brian's research contract with the Addiction Research Unit was coming to an end. We then bought Ursula Le Guin's *The Dispossessed*, which Brian read to me in two days!

I will be for ever grateful for the numerous books that Brian read me over the 17 years of our living together. Though I still don't read as many books as a true bookaholic like Brian, I find them of great importance in my life.

Though formally unemployed, I became involved in a whole range of areas: a study group on women and alcohol abuse; the Women's Theatre Group; T'ai chi; training MS counsellors (a response to the devastating news of my good friend Sal's affliction with the disease); some work with Guy and the Consortium (where I rediscovered Paul and soon resumed our relationship); assertiveness training, which I had learnt in Canada. I consequently became, to my knowledge, the first English woman to teach AT. I was to go on doing so for ten years – at least 1,000 workshops in all.

Certain incidents stand out as landmarks, such as the theatre group who created a play, *My Mother Said I Never Should*, about teenage girls, sexual curiosity, pregnancy and contraception. Daft as it now seems, I felt I couldn't take part because of my poor sight, so I wrote a number of songs which I performed live for the first months of touring, sitting on a stool at the side of the stage.

Our very first show was in a youth club in Covent Garden. At that time Covent Garden was a close-knit community, largely of Irish and Italian working people, most of them Catholic. Though I wouldn't have called our play permissive (we were trying to encourage girls to think for themselves and take responsibility for their actions), rumour had it that we were encouraging promiscuity, and an article in the local paper advised parents not to let their daughters attend this unsuitable event.

When the curtain went up the audience was 90 per cent teenage boys, ready for a good snigger. In the cramped space of the small auditorium, my knees were literally nudging the lads in the front row as I took my perch by the stage. Before the action began, it sure got going in the audience! 'Are you a virgin, Miss?' I was asked by a boy who couldn't have been more than twelve. 'What colour knickers are you wearing, Miss?' said another, pressed against my right shin. I only just managed to keep a straight face.

The banter and ribaldry kept going after the curtain went up, but what was interesting was that it related to the story and the characters. Miracle of miracles, they were all listening and taking it in. After each show we had a time for discussion. As it was clear that no one in this audience would say anything sensible in public, we invited anyone who wanted to talk to come backstage and talk with members of the cast afterwards. Rather to our surprise, a number of not very promising youths took up this invitation and showed themselves to be genuinely concerned about the whole issue of sex.

Most of the performances in schools and youth clubs were easier than this one. With girls present, the boys sometimes didn't get a look-in. The usefulness of the discussion period seemed to vary in direct relation to the quality of the youth workers or teachers present and their relationship with the kids. Where discipline was rigid, the kids didn't feel free enough to talk about their real concerns – but with the opposite ambience, a state of total *laissez faire*, even less was achieved. I still shudder when I remember an evening in a North London youth club where the atmosphere was chaotic beyond belief, with loud music blaring in the background throughout our performance and the workers making no move to do anything about it. As we wearily hauled the equipment down the stairs, they tried to justify their non-intervention on the basis of a libertarian theory of education! On reaching the car park, we found the tyres of our van slashed beyond repair. Heavy stones and bricks hurtled past our heads as we scrambled back to the relative safety of the well-lit street, still lugging our equipment. I found it incredible that the workers, having arranged for us to appear, took no responsibility for the evening or even for our safety.

Then there was the first 'Boys Rule Not OK' conference, where I had the opportunity to combine my interest in the voice with my assertiveness training. The conference was held in a converted manor house in the New Forest. Some 70 girls and young women were gathered in a circle in a huge baronial hall. The organiser, Janet Hunt, welcomed them, gave a brief introduction to the weekend and said, 'Now I shall hand you over to Frankie, who is going to get us to use our voices.'

I was quite unprepared for the outbreak of giggling and the sound of feet scampering up the stairs and under the grand piano. My career in youth work would have ended in three minutes flat, had it not been for Janet and her colleague Lois on either side of me urging me on with words like 'Keep going, Frankie! They really are interested. They're just embarrassed and unsure what is going on. Keep going. Keep going!'

One moment I would be 'calling' loudly, in desperate hope of a response coming back, and the next I was hissing under my breath to Janet and Lois 'There's no point! All I can hear is sniggering and giggling.'

'Keep going!'

Somehow I did. At the end of half an hour they were all back, soaring away at the top of their lungs. Later in the evening, when the session was over, a number of us – tutors, youth workers and girls – went out for a walk in the forest. The girls began to initiate calls. Back came the answering melodies as we stumbled through the dark, their voices resounding in the still night air. Next morning I received requests for a short voice session after breakfast, another after lunch and again before the main evening event. For years to come, I would periodically hear about girls from that course who would still sing at the drop of a hat.

I developed a 'Confidence Training' technique, specifically for use with youngsters, and used it to great effect on 15- and 16-year olds who had got into difficulties at school. One day we decided to introduce the technique to single sex groups, so the boys all went on a barge trip up the canal, leaving the girls in college with us (the arrangement was to be reversed two days later). The twelve girls clearly resented being left behind by the boys and their response to my attempts at involving them in exploring body language and rôle play was lukewarm. They just sat around, displaying the 'passive behaviour' I had been talking to them about. By mid-morning Lois and I were getting desperate.

Suddenly we realized that we had fallen into a trap which, in theory, we should be able to get out of by applying our own medicine. I took a deep breath and said, 'We seem to be getting nowhere. It's very uncomfortable for us trying to jolly you into getting off your backsides and involving yourselves. We're going to retire to the office and do something else. You can choose either to leave or to tell us why you weren't getting anything out of the session and come up with alternative suggestions. Or you can decide to go on with what we've been trying to do.'

We retired into the office, wondering how we would explain it to ILEA if half the intake decided to leave – but we couldn't have done anything else and remain consistent to our ethos and teaching. After half an hour, a girl stuck her head in and said, 'Would you like to come back and see what we've done?'

What followed was so wonderful, I only wish we could have recorded it on video. The girls took the rôle-play scenario I had suggested, and explored passivity; oozing sideways aggression, direct aggression and the polite disarming, vacuous smile. They produced the funniest, wittiest rôle plays I have ever witnessed. Lois and I were moved to tears of laughter, relief and delight at seeing the girls being so creative, so full of energy and life.

Teaching Assertion Training helped me to channel my anger and to realize the important difference between anger and aggression. Anger is a feeling: it simply *is*. Whether it is justified or not isn't the issue: if we feel it, we feel it and something needs to be done with that feeling, otherwise it will turn inwards as depression or passivity, or ooze outwards in undirected hostility. The assertive alternative we taught was finding a way to articulate these angry feelings, telling the person felt to be the 'cause' specifically what she/he had done to hurt or upset us. For me, this meant that my anger didn't have to eat me up and I didn't have to eat others up, either.

My friend Jackie Summers and I developed our idiosyncratic style of AT, which included awareness of body language, rôle play and rehearsal. A woman might, for example, tell us of a particular difficulty she was experiencing with a partner, boss or parent, and we would invite her to coach other members of the group to take the parts and play out the feared scenario with her. We would then encourage her to try out new ways of responding, based on the Assertive options. What was most extraordinary was the number of times that, returning to the group the next week, women would say things like 'It was amazing. When we met up, me all prepared, she/he [the protagonist] seemed to be quite different and the difficulty was no longer there.' This happened again and again. It's as if when we become clear inside ourselves, we unlock the other person from the pattern of relating that we've both been locked into.

The power of working on the inner landscape and its capacity to influence the world outside us became clear to me quite suddenly, when it struck me that I was responsible for so few people asking me to sing or run workshops at that time. My anxiety was preventing potential employers from getting in touch!

To this day I can't prove what I 'knew' in that moment to be true. However, I worked hard on letting go of my worries about money, security and status, which were all tied up together, and in a short while the phone started ringing; letters began falling on my doormat; the work poured in. It was as if my anxiety had created a wall around me, blocking that moment when people might think, 'Ah, yes, why not ask Frankie Armstrong to . . .?'. I've never had to worry again about enough work coming my way.

Similarly, I came to realize that on days when I was carrying a sense of frustration and resentment about needing help crossing roads or finding my way around unfamiliar tube stations, the help I ambivalently wanted was rarely forthcoming. I had enough sight to observe people scurrying by, pretending not to notice me and my white cane. On other days when I felt either cheerful or neutral, the needed help was almost always forthcoming without my having to ask for it. I had always been aware of these differences and how, once the ball was set in motion, it would spiral up or down, either making me feel immensely grateful that I had the 'excuse' for all the warming contact I got in an otherwise alienating city or, conversely, making me feel murderous towards all those self-absorbed people taking no notice of me and my needs. Then it dawned on me that I was the one who set this chain in motion. Somehow, very subtly, my inner attitude was conveying itself.

In the summer of 1975, my Voice Workshops began. During another four-week visit to the States, I had been invited to make a record by Mike Cogan, who ran Bay Records (a label that specialized for the most part in West Coast Folk and jazz). Mike said I was virtually an adopted Californian, so with Susie Rothfield, and Eric and Sue Thompson, all superb musicians, I recorded 'Out of Love, Hope and Suffering'.

Brian came too and we were able to return to the wonderful Sweets Mill Music Camp for two weeks. This time, in addition to the usual cornucopia of musicians, singers, dancers and crafts people, Ethel Raim was there. As well as her big workshops at weekends, Ethel ran daily workshops for a group of us who gathered each morning under the trees by the lake to 'Hey' and 'Yi' and croak and bleat and shake and to sing, in three-part harmony, songs that she had collected in the Balkans. With her permission I recorded a goodly number of these songs and so returned to London with three or four cassettes marked 'Ethel'.

Back in England, I enthused about the Workshops to a friend.

'How about you giving us an Ethel Raim style workshop for our group?' she asked, and this innocent question led to an evening with a group from the Singers Club which changed my whole lifestyle.

The Singers Club met at the Union Tavern in King's Cross Road. The upstairs room was nothing special but the Irish managers were friendly and loved traditional music. When I asked if I could hire the room for one evening they said they would be happy to let me have it free.

At 8 pm that Wednesday in July 1975, 23 of us gathered in a circle, sitting on wooden chairs. The only spare chair, on my left, had my cassette recorder on it, with an edited cassette of exercises and song parts that I had prepared from my recordings of Ethel's workshops – 'just in case I dry up,' I explained.

On occasions, I did. Then I would turn to my magic black box and listen to Ethel's calls to get me going again. Because I had made no bones about the fact that this was an experiment, just trying things out to see if it worked, there was a very generous spirit in the group. We laughed at some of the funny noises that ensued. After the calls and responses and warm-ups I had learned from Ethel, I taught one of the Bulgarian songs. Everyone loved it. Ethel had taught me the necessity of always giving enjoyment and never judgement, and I knew from my previous work in groups that an important part of the leader's rôle is to create a relaxed, accepting atmosphere and to be as clear as possible with the instructions.

'That was such fun!' was the consensus. 'Can we meet again next week?' I checked with the landlord. Normally the room was booked on a Wednesday, 'But Thursdays'll be fine. So we'll see you next Thursday!'

He saw us for the next year of Thursdays. The following year we moved to the Globe in Baker Street and, a year after that, to the Drill Hall, a community arts centre just off Tottenham Court Road. For three years, every Thursday evening except Christmas week, a group met to explore their voices. No money changed hands and there was no pretence that I was an 'expert', though over the years I did develop some expertise. Often it would be the participants who taught songs or suggested ways of experimenting that extended the ideas I had discovered with Ethel. My favourite phrase became 'Well, why don't we try this out and see how it feels or sounds?'

When I look back on it now, I'm surprised how slowly I seemed to learn. Some of the most important things happened by default or accident. For the first two years in the pubs we sat on chairs, but when we moved to the Drill Hall we found there weren't any. The room there was the first-floor dance studio, a space with wonderful acoustics but not a seat in sight. Sitting on the floor all evening was restricting to the voice and standing was incredibly tiring, so I hit on the idea of simulating work movements – after all, much of the workshop was based on the call and response, which originated in work chants.

That was how the famous Armstrong hoeing was born. 'Imagine we are out in the fields, hoeing the ground – forward and back, forward and back. Now I call and you simply echo my call back to me, keeping to the rhythm of the hoeing!'

We didn't of course, hoe all evening. Sometimes we sat on the floor, sometimes we swayed; finding ways to sing for two hours without chairs was put to use in a variety of good ways. All these years later, I still find people who say 'It's brilliant, moving at the same time as singing. I always thought of singing as a rather rigid activity. It's so much easier and more fun to move at the same time.' Only last week, a workshop participant said this after a warm-up. He is one out of literally thousands who have had this experience over the 16 years that have passed since that first, experimental evening in the Union Tavern.

The idea that singing involves standing or sitting still, as most of us have done in school classrooms and church choirs, seems to be of very recent origin. Throughout most of human history it's probably true that some kind of movement went with giving voice. During any given workshop, in addition to hoeing, pounding grain or tweed, treading grapes, hauling in fishing nets, scything or digging, we may dance or imagine ourselves as swaying trees, seaweed rippling under water, or even as strong, gentle gorillas, along with other human and animal images that help to liberate mind, body and voice.

The workshops are for 'singers' and 'non-singers' alike: they are designed to do away with this distinction and to have everyone enjoy expressing themselves through voice and song. I encourage the use of the open-throated style of singing found in cultures that sing in the open air, singing as naturally and spontaneously as they speak. I always ask people to bring loose, comfortable clothing, a willingness to enjoy themselves and an open mind.

I never have allowed anyone to watch a workshop without being part of it; even television crews and journalists have been requested to join in for at least half an hour before moving behind their cameras or recording apparatus. The reason I am so adamant about this is that my main rôle is to help participants not to be judgemental, either of themselves or of one another. That little nagging voice in the crown of our heads, with its insistent carpings and criticisms, is the most restricting piece of 'baggage' anyone ever brings in with them. Once we can send 'him' on his way, the work and play can truly begin. So it's crucial that no one sits on the edge in the position of an actual observer or 'judge'.

At the start of a session everyone sits or stands in a circle and introduces themselves. As I can't see clearly enough to recognize faces, I need to make connections between the sound of the voice and the name. I often begin with the question 'How would you describe your relationship with your voice? How do you feel about it – and, maybe, how does it feel about you?' I usually suggest people spend a little time reflecting on this in pairs before contributing their comments to the group. The answers give me a wide range of information very quickly. I enjoy the inventiveness these questions can inspire. 'We're playmates . . . Divorced a long time . . . Estranged and I'd like us to get together again . . . Lovers, but I make too many demands on it . . . Unreliable . . .'

At some point I'll explain my philosophy and approach. 'I've come to believe that singing and dancing are part of what it means to be human. There is a need to express ourselves through the body and voice. By "singing" I mean expressing ourselves through sound and melody, with or without words; by "dancing" I mean moving for the joy of it.'

I will point to the fact that all small children sing and dance; all so-called primitive cultures (rural and tribal) involve everyone in singing, chanting and dancing. We all come into the world with an innate capacity to express ourselves in this way. If you are born into a society that assumes you can sing, then you can sing. Singing is part of our birthright.

It is only in our present culture that so many people get told as children that they can't sing, they're 'tone-deaf', and the label sticks. Anyone so labelled is bound to get anxious and tense about singing, and this tensions makes it difficult to listen and to really hear sounds and pitches: all you hear when you listen with this kind of tension is your own panic. I know, because it has happened to me. In front of TV cameras I have sometimes been so nervous that I couldn't hear the note of my pitch pipe and had to launch into a song hoping I wouldn't fall off the top or bottom of my range.

Many teachers seem to use limited and unimaginative methods of testing whether their pupils can 'sing in tune' or not. The best way to encourage children to hear pitch and melody is through listening to another voice, pitched at a timbre the children can relate to – not a piano, which sounds nothing like a child's voice and is therefore much harder to translate into the same note. To the untrained ear, differences in timbre can sound like differences in pitch and this is very confusing. Even with the voice, since it is such a flexible instrument, the same note can be made to sound very different according to the timbre, or vocal colour, the singer decides to use. To make this point in a workshop I will sometimes illustrate it by taking one note and varying its timbre so that it sounds deeper, higher, rounder or more sinewy, according to the way I use my body and imagination – yet it remains at exactly the same pitch.

So the reason why a child may be designated a non-singer often has nothing to do with vocal and musical potential. I've heard so many wonderful, tuneful voices from people who were told that they were tone-deaf as children, demonstrating that the problem lay with the labeller and not with the labelled. And in our competitive educational system, those of us who are told we have 'good' voices also inherit a problem: from that moment on it is 'Am I going to be chosen for the solo? Will I get the high note? Will I ever be good enough?'

I feel it is valuable to help people realize they are not to blame for feeling they have, as they think, 'a bad voice'. Our voices are such an intimate part of ourselves that criticism of the voice can be felt as criticism of our whole selves, especially when we are young.

Releasing the voice, especially having people accept and enjoy their own sounds, often has very powerful effects. I wonder if it's partly because it is through using our voices that we have our first experiences of potency or impotence? The awakening baby, feeling the need for attention, attracts her mother or carer by the use of her voice. This could go some way towards explaining why, for some people, making sound has effects way beyond the obvious and conscious.

A workshop usually begins with a gentle, non-threatening loosening up of body and voice. We may imagine we are calling a long-lost friend across a busy street, or hollering our wares in the market place. Before long, I'll add a simple, rhythmic movement: my favourite is still hoeing.

At some point I'll always mention that the accuracy of the notes isn't what is important: it's the *quality* I'm interested in. 'We either keep the lid on or let the sound out freely. I'm encouraging you to do the latter. If that means you don't hit the same note as me, that's fine – it will be a harmony!' The relieved laughter that invariably follows this remark is a measure of how many people who come to workshops are anxious about their ability to 'get the notes right'.

During the day (or days, in longer workshops) there will be exercises to soften the lips, tongue and jaw, relax the throat, soften ribs, expand easy breathing and strengthen the use of abdominal wall muscle. We may use actual songs as well as free chants. When we start to focus on creating improvised harmonies, I'll say something along the lines of 'We're on a journey of discovery and it would help if we all, even me, respond to whatever comes out of our mouths with an attitude of "That was interesting!" Because if we respond with "Oh, that wasn't right!" or "That sounded awful!" we are blocking our learning. If we can look on this as a journey of discovery, nothing need be wasted. Everything will help us to learn and learning is a never-ending process.'

I'll say how, for me, harmonies are primarily about relationship. They are culturally formed: there are African style harmonies, Balkan style harmonies, western classical harmonies, Aboriginal harmonies. 'So we can experiment and try out many kinds of harmony: the only time it's *not* going to be a harmony is when you go off and do your own thing without listening and relating to what others are doing.'

It still amazes me that within hours a group of strangers, many of whom claim not to be able to sing or hold a tune, can create an improvisation with beautiful, inventive shifts of harmonies and rhythms. Somewhere in our psyches must be this 'knowledge', the equivalent of the linguist's idea of 'deep structures'. If they exist for language, which is one way of organizing sound and meaning, then why not for melodic sounds too?

In some workshops I'll play some of my tapes of ethnic singing. I owe so much to so many people, often unnamed on records and tapes. These recordings are a witness to my sources of inspiration. One of my favourites is of black prisoners in Texas, chopping trees and singing with a heartfelt longing for freedom and their loved ones. Another is of two women in Mongolia singing to the sheep and goats as they milk them: to encourage the goats, they make a wonderful blubbery sound with their lips and sing with glorious disregard of what would be considered acceptable harmonies in the bourgeois west. Sometimes I have Scottish women shrinking tweed or Macedonian women hoeing. Work songs are such a clear indication of the link between body and voice. When one listens to these tribal or rural communities involved in their vigorous action and energetic song, it's inconceivable that what's going through their heads could be 'Oh dear, I wonder if I'm singing in tune/correctly/ acceptably?' Listening to them is an encouragement to dismiss our nagging internal critics.

It is of course impossible to say what the outcome of a workshop will be for a particular person, but most of the time, most people seem to feel good about the experience. Many report that they feel more 'connected' and 'integrated' by the end. Many remark on the sense of shared creation and the feeling of communion that comes from singing together.

For individual participants to get the best out of my workshops and reach the particular experience that is there for each of them, the essential key is to come with a mind as free as possible from expectations. On one occasion, I was running a six-day session with 30 people, many (though not all) from theatrical backgrounds. On the first day, a Monday, I was informed that one participant had phoned to say that she wouldn't be able to join us until Tuesday. Let us call her Beverly.

She arrived the following morning and seemed to join in readily enough. As I always do with longer workshops, I had structured it so that on each day from Tuesday onwards we had time for physical warm-ups related to voice projection, improvisations, songs and time for 15-minute 'individual attention' sessions for anyone who wanted one.

The final individual session that day was with Sue, a theatre director who worked in youth drama. She had been told from childhood that she was tone-deaf and couldn't sing. After some call and response work with me, she went on to improvise in the middle of the circle with the rest of us providing a gentle chant as her springboard. She began with very strong, major melodies which gradually transformed into lyrical and poignant phrases. Both the melodies and the quality of her voice were very moving. The improvisation came to a natural close and she burst into tears. 'I never thought I could make such beautiful sounds!'

Next day, Wednesday, one of the men asked, would I mind if he used his individual time to work on something he knew to be highly charged emotionally? I said that was fine by me. My only rule is no violence to persons or property: after that, I'm willing to take anything on board. Let us call him David. He opted for the last slot of the day, which always left half an hour or so for the group to end collectively.

When it came to David's turn he had us all kneeling or sitting in a close circle. He told us of a personal tragedy some years earlier, when he had been living in the city we were in: being back and staying with his family had revived some powerful feelings around the death of a child. He said 'I would simply like to have the help of the group to voice my grief.'

We began the age-old custom of keening. The sounds rose and fell, swelled louder and died away. David's sorrow affected us all and we sobbed and wept through the simple melodies that arose spontaneously. After some time David stopped crying and said simply 'Thank you. That was a great help, though I know I need to do masses more of it.'

The group then began to improvise gently with a quiet melodic phrase, from which anyone who wanted to could create an individual improvisation and be heard, then meld back into the totality of sound. Before the end David had begun to create soft, haunting, yet peaceful melodies with which the day's session drew to a close. I had been very moved, not only by David's individual session but by several others – a woman singing John Pole's 'Mr Fox', which is one of my favourite songs; another feeling confident enough to teach us all a song in harmonies. Full of all this richness, I went to get into my shoes and collect my belongings.

At this moment Beverly approached me. 'Can I talk to you about something, Frankie?' I said she could and to my astonishment she said, 'I'm afraid I've come to the wrong type of your workshops. I came because friends of mine had been to one of your weekends and said it was a life-transforming experience. You see, I'm a therapist and what I'm interested in is sound and healing and how to use sound to explore emotions. I think what I've seen you do with people these past two days has been very valuable, but it obviously isn't the same sort of thing that you did on the weekend my friends went to.'

I was open-mouthed, but luckily I wasn't rendered totally speechless. I asked if she had read the publicity for the workshop. When she confessed that she hadn't, I said that reading the publicity before an event was always a good idea: nevertheless, the workshop her friends attended would have been in essence the same as this one and it would have been through these same procedures that they came to their experiences. I suggested that the expectations she came along with had blinded her to what was going on under her nose and that she talk to Sue or David or someone else who had had an individual session, as they were much more qualified than me to talk about the effects of what we had just been doing. 'Everyone here is free to take from the experience what is right for them. I don't impose this in any way.'

At this point her tack changed and she said 'My problem is that my voice always gets stuck in my throat. I'm still having that difficulty.'

I then told her we had spent much of the first day on physical exercises and imagery that encouraged participants to feel able to sing 'through' their throats and not 'with' them. I always do this as there is very little chance of achieving melodic expression of emotion unless the throat can release and open. My suggestion was that she use her individual session to work on this.

To her credit, Beverly asked for her individual time on the Friday morning and I took her gently through all the stages I had taken the whole group through on the Monday. Gradually she began to produce sounds that were very beautiful with a haunting mixture of strength and gentleness. She said it felt remarkably different from usual, allowing her to feel 'all connected up'. I was relieved and delighted. She then asked if she, too, could do an improvisation in the middle of the circle. At first the sound and the melodies, though interesting, were still a bit *angst*-laden, but gradually a lighter quality came into her voice, her movements softened into a rhythmic dance and she ended on a note of joyful abandon. She ran over to me and gave me a big hug, grinning broadly and saying in an excited voice 'Oh, that was just wonderful!' Maybe it was not life-transforming, but it certainly felt as if a rather earnest and worthy woman had been able to soften up, loosen up and enjoy herself.

I am not one of those voice teachers who feels they can change the world with what they do, but it does feel worthwhile. It's rewarding to hear how many people use aspects of my work as part of their voice and singing workshops and classes. I'm particularly pleased when I hear about those who work with people with special needs finding that they can adapt my work for use with their groups.

The strength of what I offer, as compared with the formal, western tradition of musical training, is that it comes from a different starting point – a conviction that we all have it in us to produce strong, beautiful sound, if we can only connect with our deep feelings and let go of the inhibitions and constraints of our social conditioning.

An image I use to help people get in touch with this authentic inner self is of sound rising from the earth, through the soles of the feet and up through the body, to be released through a free and open throat. A woman recently said how she loved this emphasis on a connection with the earth, adding 'I have no desire to be a higher being!' Her remark echoed some of my own reservations about a lot of New Age concepts and language, which I find too ethereal for comfort. The truth is that I'm not very interested in high standards. I'm interested in deep standards.

The workshops have given me some of my most intense moments of joy at the sheer beauty and power of the human voice. I feel a great debt to the many people who have organized them, as well as the thousands who, by taking part, have been my teachers.

Part of me is consistently surprised at the 'success' that has taken me across the world from that tentative beginning in a London pub room. I still find myself a trifle nervous at the start of a workshop, as I hope I always shall. If I were ever to take 'success' for granted, I would be on dangerous ground.

I'm aware that encouraging people to open up to the possibilities of their melodic voices may also open them up to past joy or distress, to their imagination, their emotional expressivity and an authentic personal power they may never have glimpsed before. In a funny way, it is through my own limitations as a visually impaired, unaccompanied singer with a modicum of formal musical training, that I've found such freedom through the voice and am therefore able to encourage others to do likewise.

I realize that I am also drawing on those years of social work and group work, though more by osmosis than conscious intent. Part of what I offer is a sort of fearlessness about what people may bring to the groups. Participants have wept, screamed, found themselves totally silent and literally climbed up walls as they found themselves in touch with old, repressed events that bring pain and/or anger. My job is somehow to contain and allow all this to happen and then get the person and the group back to voicing and singing. After all, I have deliberately chosen to call them 'Voice Workshops', not voice therapy.

One of the great traps is the desire to 'rescue' people from their distress and 'make it better'. When I am faced with someone in distress it's not necessarily clear to me what is needed, but I have learnt that if I allow myself and them time to listen both between and inside ourselves, the answer will unfold. Many years ago, I remember John Southgate saying 'When you're running a group, especially if it and you are getting stuck, then trust what emerges from your unconscious. However unconnected or bizarre the thoughts and images that come into your mind, trust that they have arrived there for a reason and use them.'

I have followed this advice, and find that if I give myself and the other person this stillness and listening, then somehow an idea or an image will come into my mind which enables me to suggest the next move. To the group this stillness can seem as if I don't know what to 'do' next. My greatest difficulty then can be with participants who want to 'rescue' the person who may be weeping or screaming or just standing there, numb. These eager 'rescuers' can be more difficult than the initial 'problem'. If I can allow the person in distress to feel contained, safe and recognized, I hold this to be sufficient. We may then, together, find a simple way through to a sense of peace, resolution and even celebration, which can make for some of the most moving and aesthetic-ally powerful moments in the workshop.

Over the years of intense involvement with voice, I've become more and more impressed by the mystery that lies within and behind this robust yet fragile instrument. Though our whole body, imagination and expressivity are needed to 'give voice', the actual making of the sounds involves the larynx with its vocal folds which, vibrating with air/breath and amplified in our resonance cavities, combine to create all the sounds we humans are capable of. I'm so often made aware of the potent connections we make between the physical act of voicing and the way we feel about things. The evidence is in our everyday language: I felt choked up . . . it stuck in my gullet . . . I just couldn't swallow it . . . I could have bitten off my tongue . . . It's little wonder that our throats sometimes become a sticking point in moments of conflict. Hence, helping to free and soften up the area of the throat and jaw and to deepen breathing can be powerfully therapeutic. My focus, however, remains on the sound itself. What I feel drawn to is helping people rediscover the joy and power of singing. As a person with 34 years' experience of singing publicly, 22 years in social and group work, and certain abilities I was 'forced' to develop through losing my sight, I have come to feel that the work is tailormade for me.

Chapter 13

After my experience in the States I was quite sure that I didn't want to be a full-time singer, though I still got periodic bookings with folk clubs. I could have found an agent and put all my energies into 'making it', but I knew the lifestyle was too ephemeral for me – arriving in a town or city, performing, and then having to move on to the next. Some people love it and, like the renowned folk singer Martin Carthy, seem to thrive, keeping an openness and a humanity which I know the life would have knocked out of me.

There were two main settings in which I performed – folk clubs and the Women's Movement. Each in its own way threw up conflicts and contradictions for me. The folk clubs had two factors that I found difficult: they invariably met in pubs, which meant singing in an atmosphere affected by smoking and drinking, and the greater proportion of performers (including paid guests) were men; the clubs had a 'male ambience'. As a female guest, I was already in a minority; as a singer who sang mostly of women's experience, I was a rarity and something of a challenge to the average folk club audience. I probably preached a bit, but even at my most militant I don't think I lost my sense of humour: I actually learnt to enjoy the repartee that sometimes got going when I was on stage.

I remember one evening at a club on the waterfront in Bristol when an old salt in the audience called out 'What's all this with women's complainings? How about some love songs?' I pointed out that I had sung 'The Bird in the Bush'. This immediately drew the retort 'That weren't love, that were lust!'

I didn't mind this kind of barracking, done with humour and generosity. What I did find hurtful was that people would corner me at the end of an evening – usually men, but occasionally women – and accuse me of being embittered because I couldn't get a man! I could have silenced them with 'As a matter of fact, I've been living with the same man now for seven/nine/eleven years!' But that would not have answered the most disturbing aspect of this kind of thinking; resorting to personal attack rather than tackling the issues raised by the songs.

The classic challenge was 'Why sing all these songs about women?'. I would cheerfully reply, 'I bet it would never occur to you to ask Johnny Collins or Martin Carthy or the Boys of the Lough why they sing primarily about men's lives and men's ways of looking at the world!'

One evening I was singing at a folk club in Hereford. (The smaller the town, the more of a stir my performances tended to create.) I had finished the evening, as I often did, with 'I'm Gonna Be an Engineer'. As I came off stage a man in his sixties, black beret on white head, advanced towards me with his hand held out in a forceful gesture. I wondered for a moment if he was going to hit me, but he grasped my hand and pumped it vigorously up and down saying 'Thank you! Thank you so much for this evening! It's so important, the things you're saying and getting us to think about. Unless we can find different ways of relating to one another, men and women, nation and nation, there's not much hope for us!' But it was mostly women who came up and said how moved and excited they had been by what I had to say and sing.

Out of the discomfort and challenge of singing both women's songs in folk clubs and traditional songs within the Women's Movement, I wrote a song that, I feel, holds as true now as it did in 1977 when I wrote it. It is called 'Women of My Land'.

Down streams of centuries grown old, across the seas of
time
You wove your love and hopes and fears into tune and
rhyme.

You spun your sufferings into song to help you to survive
In factories and farms and mines, to keep your soul alive.

And now I try and sing your songs, in hope to understand
Who I am and who you were, women of my land.

At evenings when the spring was young, you sang wild
songs of love
And called your lover far or near a blackbird or a dove.

Often children brought you joy but sometimes brought
you pain,
For lovers left and you could find no shelter from your
shame.

Your songs could tell a crafty tale, full of laughter and wit,
You turned the tables on the men and the biter found
himself bit.

Some of you were bold as brass, said 'To hell with custom
and law'
And dressed as soldier and sailor boys, you went off to
war.

Together you sang in farms and factories, arm in arm you
strolled down the street.
Your voices rang, on the picket line you sang, in time to
the tramp of your feet.

But always they said your place was to serve – husband,
master and King.
You tried to defy this centuries-old lie, and one of your
ways was to sing.

So now I try and sing your songs in hopes to understand
Who you were and who I am, women of my land.

And when I think how many of you died, so young in
labour and pain,
These songs I sing are the tribute that I bring and make me
link in your chain.

All in all, I was at one of the busiest, most rewarding points in my life. But I began to feel a need for space and stillness. I felt driven by my social and political conscience: whenever I was asked to sing or lend my support to a cause I believed in, it felt irresponsible to say no and 'let people down'. I felt uncertainty and fear about what was happening to my sight, but this wasn't the central issue: there were times when I became quite desperate as I sensed myself being driven, crowded, pushed into action by the demands around me. Yet there I was, also feeling a strong need to give time to the inner world, to the roots of the creative.

I felt myself torn and confused by this conflict as I approached the end of my 35th year. And then a friend suggested that I should see the wonderful Buntie Wills, a Jungian therapist.

An appointment was made and on February 1st, 1977, I made the first of many hundreds of visits to Cunningham Place. I rang the bell and waited, wondering what significance this meeting would have. I heard footsteps coming down the staircase, the door opened and I could see enough to tell that Buntie had snowy white hair. I sensed that she was still beautiful – an impression that was corroborated by many people and especially by Brian, who thought her exquisite. She welcomed me with a hug that was neither invasive nor artificial and led me up to her first-floor waiting room where she settled me, saying she would be ready shortly.

The room, which I explored, had plants and pictures hanging on the walls, several chairs and a small table covered with books, leaflets and pamphlets. The leaflets spanned a range of subjects, including ecology, alternative medicine, creative and expressive workshops, education, holistic retreats and holidays. Then I heard talk and laughter at the top of the stairs and a pair of feet coming down them. Buntie reappeared and invited me into her working room. The lighting was soft, glowing from a table lamp, and I could smell flowers. She sat me down on a wing-back chair covered in deep purple velvet ('home' to so many of us for many years), sat down herself and said 'Now, dearest, tell me, what gives your life meaning?'

Buntie was never one to skirt the key questions. I felt that she enjoyed my answers. Now and then she added some of her own enthusiasms to affirm mine. What clinched it for me was the moment when she leant forward and grasped my hand warmly saying 'I do love people with passion!'

She did, indeed. She had a passionate nature herself, which she combined with serenity. Buntie embodied the balance I was seeking, the still point between turning out towards the world and turning towards the deep waters within. I was to see her every week for many years.

Part of what I wanted to find in myself could be described as 'being more fully and richly womanly.' I wasn't sure exactly what this meant, but Buntie pointed out how my confidence, though strong enough in many aspects of my life, didn't extend so consistently to my sense of myself as a woman. I had once been more sure of my sensuality, my attractiveness (not in the style of glamorous magazines, but a deeper sureness of a soft, strong, feminine quality) and I seemed to have lost this in the process of becoming more active and successful out in the world. Now it was as if a whole other process had to be lived through before I could get this quality back.

Shortly after I began seeing Buntie, I found myself having extraordinarily vivid dreams, full of colour and imagery, and incredibly inventive, often with a strong sense of humour. When working in Sweden in the summer of 1977, I stayed with my gay singer friend, Jan Hammarlund, in a gay and lesbian community in Gottenburg. I proceeded to dream that I was sleeping on a *camp* bed with beautiful pale lavender sheets. Outside the window was a Gothic cathedral with a spire reaching way up into the heavens. At the time Jan presented the epitome of the soulful artist – poetic, spiritual and for ever out of my reach: that spire was an apt symbol for him. What a glorious combination of punning and metaphor in one brief dream!

I suppose I was feeling in something of a non-creative

limbo. I was enjoying singing but had hit a sticky patch with the development of the weekly voice workshops. I had begun to feel grossly inadequate. I was permanently carrying around a little judge in my head who kept wagging his skinny finger at me and telling me that I wasn't good enough. I could sing, but I was neither rich nor famous. I did this funny thing on Thursday evenings, getting people to call and sing a bit, but pretty well anybody could do that. I found myself spending a lot of time at home on my own, feeling at a loose end with no clear sense of direction.

One morning I turned on the radio and found myself doing something I had never done before: I compared myself unfavourably with each and every person speaking on the Radio 4 *Today* programme. 'They've been to university/ written a book' and 'they know about economics/ are really doing something to change the world for the better.' Whatever they did, it all served to contrast with my inadequacy.

I had dreams in which I found myself in court rooms with bewigged judges. I met swarthy men wielding guns and dark-suited men who led me up steps, higher and higher. In one dream a dark man with slicked-down hair led me to the top of the Empire State Building and, as we sat on the flat roof looking down at the traffic and the tiny people, he produced some eggs which I proceeded to roll over the edge, possibly to land on the unsuspecting pedestrians below.

I wrote these dreams down. At my next session Buntie read through the one about the eggs. She asked, 'Were they raw or cooked?'

'Hard-boiled,' I replied, walking into the trap.

'I wouldn't like to be at the receiving end of that hard-boiled character's eggs!' she laughed, but she said it sharply enough for me not to miss her meaning. The dream clearly told me that from my lofty viewpoint I had been doling out some pretty harsh judgements to those I saw as beneath me.

A later dream was set in the house where I had lived with my parents from the age of six to 21. I was in the kitchen when in through the front door and down the hallway came a young gangster figure. Although I was scared, I faced him and asked him to leave. He went back into the front hall and I went into the front room, where I found a young girl of about four singing and dancing. I said I was going down the road to the shop, to buy her some sweets. As I went out, I found the young man lolling against the door frame and to my surprise gave him a kiss on the cheek as I walked past him. His face broke out into a gentle, radiant, beaming smile and I half danced, half ran up the garden path, feeling a tremendous sense of lightness and relief.   '

Though I remembered this feeling when I woke, it was several weeks before I became aware of a profound inner shift – the gradual lifting of something disturbing and distressing that had 'possessed' me quite intensely for months, but which I realized had lurked about for much longer, maybe all my life. I always had a tendency to intolerance which had become more pronounced after I took Marxism and the Women's Movement on board.

Through my work with Buntie I had been slowly recognizing this, and the harsh judges and threatening gangsters were my dream symbols of it. Having acknowledged this, I could now let go, becoming at once less threatened and less threatening. Buntie did not interpret these dreams: rather, she led me to tease out what my unconscious was trying to help me face. I could be a very slow learner, but she never forced her perceptions on me. As I became more generous to myself, I began to be more generous to others. I can still be intolerant of other people, but now I'm less likely to become obsessed and 'hooked in' by these feelings.

It was after this painful period, when I was beginning to feel more generous towards myself as well as others, that I began to look at my rôle as performer and runner of workshops.

I had a summer break from therapy and then returned to Buntie with a folder full of dreams including a series about the performer/audience relationship. One dream had me singing to a large crowd from the top of a tall pedestal. In another, I was singing from behind to the backs of a floating audience as we were all punted down canals on rafts. In yet another, I was on a huge stage and the microphone went completely dead so that no one could hear me. In several I was singing with a band and came in on embarrassingly wrong notes.

In the workshop dreams other disasters occurred: the most frequent was the slow, silent departure of participants from the circle, until I was left on my own without having seen the process taking place – a complete nightmare.

Buntie and I explored these dreams together and her insight helped me to let go of some of the pride and, hence, the fear that can so easily beset a stage performer. It is less important to impress and prove anything than it is simply to share songs I love with the audience. It sounds straightforward, but to do this took a good deal of self-searching. It still does.

Similarly, in the workshops I was gradually able to let go of any sense that I needed the participants to prove what a wonderful teacher I was and instead allow them responsibility for their own learning at their own pace. I managed to stop importing my egotistical needs into the group, and to stay vigilant, aware of my own responses and how to use them appropriately.

Buntie and I addressed in detail the issue of control. As an intelligent, creative woman, I had to establish a strong identity and to demand of life and others that they allow me to do this. I had to control my own life, and to do so, I could be somewhat invasive and demanding. In that purple chair, I struggled – as many others did – to create a new balance for myself. The battle to feel in control had been necessary, but it was now, in some way, a barrier to entering the next phase of my life.

Again, I worked through this problem in dreams. I was by now in my late 30s and I had not been physically sick since I was six, when I ate too much chocolate while staying with a friend and vomited all over the pristine bed cover. I had been so mortified by the incident that I determined never to let it happen again. Now I started to vomit in my dreams and –

eventually – it gradually became less unpleasant. Then, after a dream in which I had been thoroughly sick, Buntie gave me a big hug and I realized I felt just wonderful. I had lost my fear of vomiting. As if to test me out, I then began to have strange stomach cramps which frequently made me vomit. I had tests, but there was no apparent reason for them and they stopped as mysteriously as they'd begun.

So I gradually came to feel less driven, less anxious, less overweeningly responsible. One afternoon I turned up at Cunningham Place for my weekly appointment. Buntie opened the door and said 'Frankie, what are you doing here?'

'I've come for my appointment, of course,' I replied.

'But dearest, you're at the wrong time on the wrong day!'

She swept me into her arms and gave me a big hug. I could hear the twinkle in her eye. 'This is marvellous. Our work must be having its effect. It means that you're letting go of being so terribly conscientious, so responsible and predictable! I can't see you now, but if you wait till I've finished with my current sweetheart I'll make you a cup of tea and send you on your way.' Such were the unorthodox ways of Buntie Wills.

For anyone with a physical or sensory disability, the issue of control is of course tied up with the struggle for independence. Much of my compulsive efficiency was and is to do with the need always to know where things are, to keep information in my head and to have others be efficient so that it's possible for me to function. I still need to do this, but it has taken on a profoundly different feel. It is now a matter of negotiating the kind of interdependence that allows me my autonomy as a woman and an artist.

A process that unfolded more slowly, less dramatically than the others, could be described as re-membering the lost, womanly parts of myself. I began to have dreams in which older women led me down wooden steps into deep, green undergrowth. It was around this time that a friend introduced me to the Body Shop and encouraged me to have my ears pierced. Earrings more than anything symbolize an acceptance and celebration of my womanhood. As my interest in colour, fabric and design was rekindled, my jeans and sweaters gradually gave way to corduroy or silk jump suits and soft, well cut tracksuits. I began to feel able to dress to please and express myself; no longer in reaction against male-defined, feminine fashion, but celebrating myself as an attractive woman on my own terms with the affirmation and help of close women friends.

All this, predictably, resulted in a number of romantic entanglements with younger men, older men, some requited, some unrequited, but all involving me in the fantasies and projections that are an inevitable part of the poetry and pain of 'falling in love'. Buntie, who must have seen all this so many times before, remained able to support me through it all, seeing it as a necessary process. She often spoke of 'the inner marriage': how we can find the strong female and male elements in ourselves and create an inner marriage which gives us true autonomy and, at the same time, feel free to make an 'outer' partnership. I gradually felt this sense of inner relationship and completeness forming inside me.

Around 1975 I became aware each time I visited my parents in the Lakeland hills that a little more vision had departed. Views became increasingly impressionistic. In 1977, when the glaucoma in my right eye was fluctuating and not responding consistently to treatment, I would sometimes find myself overwhelmed with a sense of loss and burst out crying at unexpected times and places. I began to search desperately for some way – any way – to stop my sight deteriorating. I tried acupuncture. I tried a most extreme macrobiotic diet. I tried a combination of biofeedback, meditation and visualization. I spent thousands of pounds on in-treatments and out-treatments and fares and meals, until I had spent all my savings with no noticeable benefits. It was then that a chance encounter showed me where I needed to look next.

In June 1978, back at the Sweets Mill Festival in California, I met a young woman who had just been diagnosed as suffering from glaucoma in both eyes. She worked at an alternative health clinic and told me how a battery of alternative practitioners had begun advising her to try this and try that until her head was spinning and her financial resources were exhausted. In the end she was more frightened of her life turning into some sort of vendetta against her failing eyesight than she was of actually losing her vision. I realized that I must now search inside myself for a real acceptance of whatever might be my fate.

But with this realization came a greater sense of loss. I suppose I had been hoping that one of the many alternative treatments I tried would push back the slow shroud that was covering my one functioning eye. For several years, I had found autumn a painful season. I loved the changing colours and the misty, mellow fruitfulness. Would I still be able to see the subtly shifting hues the next time autumn came round?

Over the next few years, Buntie and I spent some time exploring my response to my increasing blindness. It was never the focal point of our work together, though we both realized it was intimately connected with the whole 'letting go' process that I needed to face and work through.

In the meantime, my cram-packed life continued. I helped the beautiful and intelligent Kathy Henderson compile the book *My Song is My Own* – the first British collection of songs, old and new, reflecting women's experience, and made a record of it. I recorded 'Nuclear Power, No Thanks' and sang for the Greenham marchers and campers. I felt very honoured when the Greenham women chose my song 'Out of the Darkness' to be on the cover of their song book.

Out of the darkness comes the fear of what's to come,
Out of the darkness comes the dread of what's undone,
Out of the darkness comes the hope that we can run
and out of the darkness comes the knowledge of the sun.

Out of the darkness comes the fear of the unknown
Out of the darkness comes the dread of bleaching bone.
Out of the darkness comes the hope we're not alone
and out of the darkness grow the seeds that we have sown.

Out of the darkness comes the fear, revenge and hate
Out of the darkness comes the dread of indifferent fate,
Out of the darkness comes the hope we're not too late
and out of the darkness come the songs that we create.

Darkness is the place of birth, darkness is the womb,
Darkness is the place of rest, darkness is the tomb.
Death belongs to life. Half of day is night.
The end won't come in darkness but a blinding flash of
light.

More Life and Love, More Work,
More Song

Chapter 14

In 1982 I took part in the Easter encircling of Aldermaston, Papworth Common and the Greenham base. It was an amazing feat of organization, the stewards spreading us around as evenly as possible and sending radio messages around the circle to report where there were still gaps. At last the word went up 'We've made it!' Up went the cheers and the brightly coloured helium balloons.

Leon Rosselson, Roy Bailey and I were working together from time to time and we had been asked to sing at Papworth Common after the encirclement. Our stage was the back of a lorry, rigged up with amplification. As we clambered up, I realized from the nature of the noise around us and from Leon and Roy's expletives that a phalanx of anarchists with their black leather clothes and red banners were at the front of the crowd. I was familiar with them from Hyde Park demos I had sung at over the years, but here they seemed to be more in evidence. I don't know to this day what I said to turn their heckling and slogan chanting into involvement, but by the end they were all singing along with 'Shall There Be Womanly Times Or Shall We Die?'

Leon's songs are now an important part of my current concert repertoire. 'Voices' is a song I sing at every opportunity. It begins:

In the stagnant squalor of a shanty town
A woman is singing
She cannot read, she cannot write her name
But the voice that lives inside her makes her strong
It calls a thousand other voices into song
It breaks the sullen silence of the sky

And wakes the ragged children who must scavenge to
survive
And shakes the soundproof citadels where paper deals are
made

A world away

I had been singing with Leon and Roy at CND-sponsored concerts and we went on to perform together in Canada and the USA and on the continent. Leon and I were also involved in a recording of songs by Brecht, 'Let No One Deceive You'.

My work in the Peace Movement led to the recording of two of my best-known songs, 'Womanly Times' and 'Message From Mother Earth'. The former was inspired by the writer Ian McEwan's line 'Shall there be womanly times or shall we die?' and from the Greenham women and Babies Against the Bomb. BAB joined me in recording them on a seminal single.

'Mother Earth' isn't one of my best written songs, but it does the job for which it was intended. With its chorus 'Remember, I give you birth, Remember Mother Earth!' it does move people. It is certainly the song of mine that has been most sung.

Although there is no longer the same dramatic focus on the Peace Movement and women's environmental movements, the number of women involved seems to me still very hopeful. Many of us are working in far more broadly based groups and local, grassroots ventures, which get comparatively little media attention. Everywhere I go I meet powerful, passionate, committed women, working away at these issues.

Early in the autumn of 1979 I was faced with a serious crisis over my sight. The pressure on my right eye, the only one with any vision, had been controlled with drops ever since that alarming day in 1971 when I had become unable to see the blossom on a tree in the course of a single walk. Now my consultant at Moorfields told me that the eye condition was getting worse, in spite of the drops, and if he didn't operate the pressure would lead to total loss of sight. So an operation was arranged, to take place on the day after the launch of

Kathy Henderson's book *My Song Is My Own*.

I had just returned from a holiday in Crete with Brian. It had been a very strange holiday, as the confidence and balance I am used to having when I walk on cliffs and mountains had deserted me and I felt real fear on our walks: my inner and outer equilibrium both felt precarious.

We launched *My Song Is My Own* with a concert at the ICA in the Mall. Kathy and I travelled in from South London together on one of those crisp, late autumn afternoons when the sun seems to illuminate the leaves like stained glass. After the sound check, Kathy and I walked briefly in St James's Park. We looked at the orange and white ducks swimming in the lake, brilliant in the last rays of the setting sun, and I said 'I'm scared. This may be the last time I see ducks, or autumn leaves, or sun dappling on water.'

Kathy was consoling, but not pitying. She said quietly that she knew I had the resources to cope with such a loss if the worst were to happen. I'll always feel grateful for her calm confidence in me at that moment.

As with many of my deepest friendships, Kathy and I came to know and trust one another partly through working together and partly through my response to her having her first baby. Kathy had delivered the manuscript of 'My Song Is My Own' just before delivery of her firstborn child. So the growth of our friendship, the development of the book and the creation of Charley all interwove.

Shortly before his birth, I wrote her a long, heartsearching letter from a family planning clinic in Brixton. I had finally decided to have a tubal ligation and was there for counselling interviews about it and to see if I could get it on the National Health. I was 39 and by now it was clear that I didn't want children. I suspect I am too selfish to make a good mother. I know I am not selfish in the usual sense of the word, but there is something very strong in me that is focused on my 'path' and that doesn't leave much room for the demands that children would make. I have unbounded admiration for those women who can develop their own creative path and also provide the full depth of relationship that children need. Writing to Kathy at the point of no return helped me to clarify the issues without feeling any need to take up a moral stance for or against having children.

Kathy's response was characteristic: she visited me in hospital on the morning after the operation and asked me if I would be Charley's godmother. She said she wanted to 'give' him to me as my child, too. She recognized that my choice had not been without its sadness: acknowledging this meant, to her, that it was a real decision. Since that day I have been privileged to share in Kathy's joy over Charley and at the subsequent arrival of Daniel and Annie, his younger brother and sister. Only a matter of weeks after publication of the book, I remember us pushing Charley as a toddler up to the park in Brixton and for an hour or so all three of us were caught up in the experience of chasing leaves, feeding ducks and watching our shadows lengthen.

Chapter 15

I continued to see Buntie once a week for several years. At one level nothing extraordinary happened. Two women sat opposite each other in a cosy first-floor flat and talked. Sometimes we sat in silence. Occasionally I wept. Mostly we just talked.

I love talking, but I'm also aware of the limitations of talking as a means to a greater sense of wellbeing and aliveness. Talking about the self can so often go round in circles and become self-indulgent, so for the most part I prefer some kind of action. I am well aware that some people regard therapy as a self-indulgent luxury. Of course it is only possible when there is sufficient affluence and in my case it wasn't a necessity. At the same time I'm in no doubt that the £12–15 a week I spent on making myself a clearer, calmer, more effective person was money well spent. The quantity of my political and social involvement has reduced, but I'm convinced that the quality has improved.

So we sat and talked. More importantly, we truly met. Buntie would say 'It's what happens in the space between us that's the important thing.' Because I always felt seen and fully accepted, I began to open up to new ways of seeing things, allowing new realizations to dawn and a new awareness to filter through.

Because of my successful therapy I decided to train as a therapist myself. After all those years in social work, it was quite a logical progression and there was something unsettled in me which was prompting me to be stretched further. I talked with Buntie about it and, after we had waded through a variety of leaflets, applied and was accepted for training with the Guild of Psychotherapists. However, life was to steer me in a different direction.

I first heard of Pat Watts from Buntie Wills. Pat, like me and long before me, had found ways of synthesizing her two major 'careers', as drama teacher and Jungian counsellor. Buntie said she was sure I would love Pat's workshops, so one day in 1980 I plucked up my courage and booked in for a day at Westminster Pastoral Foundation. It took courage because I didn't know how much I would be able to enter into these workshops or how left out I might feel through being unable to see.

It was a grey Sunday and the Circle Line was long delayed. By the time I had found the building and the top floor room I was late. Horrors! The session was already under way, so I had missed my chance to explain my situation to the group and to Pat. This was going to be a nightmare. I was sure to blunder about and make an idiot of myself. (These days I feel pretty immune to such fears, but 11 years ago I still had these feelings.)

My fears were unfounded. Pat created an opportunity to pair off with me in the next movement exercise, so I was able to explain my situation. She said she had heard about me and my work and had been delighted to see my name on the list. She gave me a chance to explain to the group before instructing us in the next exercise, but continued to partner me herself. We were to touch fingertips with our partner and begin moving, trying to create such a sensitive awareness that there was no sense that one was leading and the other following, but rather that the two moved as one. The energy current that seemed to run through our fingers and hands was such that they became warm and tingling and our 'dance' seemed rather to move us than have any conscious intent. It was a powerful start to our friendship. The group spent most of the morning improvising creation stories. As these were mostly ritualized movement and sound, I was able to join in with no difficulty.

After lunch Pat said we would spend the afternoon working on the Norse legend of Loki and Baldur. Baldur was a son of Odin and Frigg, the rulers of Asgard, the world of the gods. He had a blind brother, Hod, whom he protected and took care of. Baldur was strong, courageous and loving, and he aroused the jealousy of Loki, the evil trickster.

An old woman prophesies the death of Baldur and the downfall of the gods. Frigg, distraught, travels the length and breadth of the world extracting from each creature, each animal, human and growing thing, a promise that they will never harm her son. But she overlooks and doesn't ask the help of an unobtrusive plant, the mistletoe. Loki discovers that Frigg has missed out the mistletoe and makes a dart of it. Frigg returns to Asgard and announces that her son is safe: nothing and no one will harm him. There is great rejoicing and for fun, to prove his immunity, Baldur is bombarded with missiles. They bounce off him, leaving him unscathed. Baldur's blind brother, Hod, is seated on the edge of these celebrations, unable to join in. Loki offers him the dart, saying there is no reason why he shouldn't take his turn. He helps Hod to point the dart in Baldur's direction. The dart hits Baldur but, instead of bouncing off him as all the others have done, it pierces him and he falls to the ground dead. From this deed follows the downfall of the gods and their replacement by the human race.

Pat asked who would like to play the named rôles. It seemed that my fears of being unable to join in fully were strangely unfounded, as the story offered me a rôle in which my feared disadvantage would be a positive advantage. I was both drawn to and scared of playing the blind brother, Hod. To have one's blindness the cause of the death of a beloved brother and ultimately the destruction of the entire family and pantheon of gods was a heavy burden to take on. Symbolically, it was my worst fantasy. I offered to play Hod. For all my fears of what this might stir up, I already felt a trust in Pat and knew she would see me through, whatever might arise. Her manner was strong, calm and soundly earthed.

It was an extraordinary enactment. I don't think this was especially because of me, but I did add to the dramatic truth of the storytelling. Initially, the group worked on separate sections of the story. For the entire afternoon, we all brought such focus and imagination to bear on what we were doing that when we came to enact the complete story, it was riveting. I found the final scene intensely painful. The moment when the dart struck my beloved brother and a deathly silence took the place of all the singing and laughter was almost unbearable.

'What's happened? What's going on? Why the silence?' I pleaded desperately.

The fact that I knew the story intellectually made no difference to the powerful feelings that swept over me. My nightmare: screeching brakes, silence, what's happened? Where's Brian/Mum/Dad? It might be on a steep mountain-side, a flight of steps, who knew where or how, but I would be left without knowing what had happened and what my rôle was in the dreadful accident.

When the enactment was over it was clear that I had been deeply shaken and moved by the experience, yet in a strange way I also felt stronger and calmer for having faced and acted out this nightmare. Pat could see this. She came over to me. 'Frankie, it's had a powerful effect on us all and it must have for you, especially. Thank you for that. Are you feeling all right about it?'

I assured her that, distressing as it had been, it had actually left me feeling glad that I had taken the part of Hod.

'It's quite extraordinary,' she said. 'when I was planning the session early this morning this particular myth popped into my mind, though I haven't done it for a long time now. I knew you were on the list of participants, but I had no idea you were visually handicapped. When I realized the coincidence, I sensed it would be okay to go ahead with the story I'd planned. I felt you would do what you needed and that I could trust that.' Coincidence or synchronicity, it meant that Pat and I discovered a mutual trust and respect from our first meeting.

In the autumn of 1981, Brian and I joined a 10-week evening course that Pat was running at WPF on Tuesdays. There were about twelve of us and the group worked really well from the outset. We improvised and enacted *Perseus and*

Medusa, a strange, open-ended Noh tale, and Bushmen stories including *The Water Jug Boy* and *The Boy, the Lion and the Storm Tree*. I can still recall each dramatization and the power of the imagery evoked. No one in the group allowed inhibitions or embarrassment to get in the way of total involvement in our explorations.

Because Brian and I were used to using our voices, Pat encouraged us to use sounds whenever possible and this in turn encouraged everyone else. I only discovered later, from Pat, that these sessions were a turning point in terms of the use of sound in her work.

Something crystallized for me during those ten weeks. On Tuesday evenings I acted, sang and danced with Pat's group – twelve people who knew nothing about one another, but felt a closeness and trust that were strong and tangible through our shared task, evenings which never failed to leave me feeling enriched and more alive at the end. And on Wednesdays, at my first term with the Guild of Psycho-therapists, a group of about the same size sat around talking about ourselves, our thoughts and feelings, about therapy, groups, and what it felt like in this particular group. Inevitably such a group, by focusing on its own processes, gets caught up in frustrations, paranoia and other very negative experiences, which provide valuable insight to trainee psychotherapists. We did learn from it, but I began to question whether this was really what I, personally, needed.

Pat started to come to my voice workshops and absolutely loved them. At precisely the same moment, we hit on the idea of running groups together and so the workshops 'Voice and Movement Towards the Enactment of Myth' were born. I count myself fortunate to have co-led groups with Pat: she is wise, funny, iconoclastic and imaginative, having led a far from conventional life. I love the stories and myths we have worked with. Through using body and voice to give them shape, they have come alive and dance in my soul.

Towards the end of my first year of training I had a dream which clearly showed me my path.

I dreamt that I was walking down a light, airy corridor and

met my Swedish friend, Lena. She was wearing an exquisite jacket made of multicoloured patches, arranged in wonderful designs. Its vibrancy and beauty were electrifying. Lena said, 'I can take you to the shop where you can buy all the wools and patterns, if you like.'

I replied, 'I'm sorry, but just now I'm on my way to a seminar with a very eminent psychologist and philosopher.'

We parted and I went to the seminar. About a dozen of us were sat in a circle on comfortable chairs. The teacher was in his sixties, thin and very wise looking, and talked with great erudition. His talk was truly fascinating, but when it was time for questions at the end I got up and said simply 'Thank you, I have enjoyed it immensely, but I need to be somewhere else.'

I walked back down the corridor and met Lena once again. We found ourselves in a room full of the most glorious wools, tapestries and fabrics and I knew that my path must be towards creating shapes and designs with colour.

When I woke up it was quite clear to me that I should now leave the Guild of Psychotherapists. They were very understanding and promised me a place on the course if ever I changed my mind. It was a nice thought, but I can't see that I ever will.

Chapter 16

My enjoyment of Pat's myth enactments no doubt influenced me in my decision to embark on a theatrical adventure shortly after I left the psychotherapy training. I was running some workshops for Graeae Theatre Company, the only professional company for actors with disabilities, when I heard they were planning a production to tour India. When it was suggested that I join the company for the tour, I juggled eagerly with my diary dates to make room for the rehearsal period.

The show was being directed by a young director, Nigel Jamieson, who was excited at the prospect of my joining them. We arranged to meet and hit it off immediately: we have remained friends ever since.

Nigel arranged for the team of actors to meet up in the summer, before we began rehearsals, for us to get some idea of each other and for him to ask us for pointers to the issues that would be explored in the play. Graeae had been invited by the Indian Government, through Interlink, to put on a play about disability with the purpose of raising awareness within India and helping change prevailing attitudes. Nigel explained that his approach would involve us in some non-naturalistic styles, using physical work, voice, song and symbolic imagery, with elements from the circus and vaudeville as well as the naturalistic.

We were a most extraordinary group. I had heard about Nabeil Shaban and found him as electrifying as I had been led to believe. Nabs has brittle bones and is very small and confined to a wheelchair, but the term 'wheelchair-bound' is peculiarly inappropriate to him. He moves his wheelchair with the same expressivity as his face and hands: it is simply an extension of himself. Jag Plah, an Indian with cerebral palsy, is equally extraordinary. His family came to England when he was six, largely to find opportunities for Jag. Jag has rare charm and exceptional clarity of perception. Eli Wilkie, a beautiful woman with a fine singing voice, had severe muscular dystrophy which meant that she, too, was in a wheelchair, with her by then very curved spine causing her to sit with her face always tilted. In spite of this, she sang like a lark. Jim Gibbon, also small with a severely curved spine, could manage some time out of the wheelchair so long as the activity wasn't too tiring. I had convinced him at a workshop that being small didn't mean he couldn't sing strongly and he turned out to have a great voice.

At our first meeting in the summer we were all excited about the tour. We bristled with ideas and sparked off one another, engendering such a sense of anticipation that we could hardly bear to wait for rehearsals to begin in the autumn. The plan was for Nigel to write the show in the intervening time, but when we all gathered in Aldershot in October, Nigel said 'I started writing, but then I realized it was ridiculous. How could I, an able-bodied person, with no experience of what it's like to be disabled, write a play for all of you about your experiences? It's going to be one hell of a rush, but the only thing we can do is devise the whole thing together!'

Nigel knew the risk was enormous with only four weeks before we were due to leave for India. Four weeks is a short period to rehearse a scripted play, let alone devise and rehearse something from scratch. My respect for him as an artist and a person came from my initial admiration for his willingness to 'sit in the void' with all the uncertainties and anxieties that involves, rather than do the safer thing, knowing it to be patronizing and no way to tell our truth.

Our starting point was physical warming-up exercises and improvisations, to give Nigel an idea of what we could do physically. This was my first encounter with the style of work developed by Jacques LeCoq. Out of this emerged wondrous things. Who would ever have imagined a spastic juggling, or doing one of those theatrical falls, flat on the face – or Nabs riding his wheelchair with the whirling, rearing, plunging motions of a Roman charioteer, and me spinning my white cane like a drum majorette? We had a wonderful time testing out all the possibilities, pushing our limitations to their outermost boundaries and finding some images of great theatricality in the process.

Nigel trusted us to work within the margins of safety and left us to define what these were: a lesser director would have called a halt long before. We began exploring scenes from our own lives, setting up naturalistic improvisations and finding imagery to express the struggles, frustrations and triumphs that, to some degree, we had all experienced. By week two we began to see a shape emerging. We would tape our improvisations and next morning Nigel would turn up with a scripted version. Then he would say 'Frankie, could you write us a song for this point in the script before tomorrow?' Somehow I did. We were all being pushed to our limits, yet somehow we got the show together on time.

At last the big day arrived and we settled into our seats on the Air India Jumbo, eating curry and feeling that the pressures had all been worthwhile. In Bombay city we found ourselves booked into a luxury hotel overlooking a beach with palm trees. A traditional wedding was in progress when we arrived and we were greeted with garlands of fragrant flowers, the women in our party being invited to have our hands painted with intricate patterns of henna. We visited Calcutta and Delhi and saw many amazing sights. The best part of each visit was the time spent in the special schools for spastics, where the quality of the work and of the relation-ships struck us as soon as we entered the door. The children were, of course, from middle-class homes: we were dis-tressed to see poor spastic children begging in the streets, but this sad fact couldn't detract from the quality of the work we saw in the special schools.

In every city there were receptions with local officials, but we also made sure that we visited the local flea markets. The sight of three small people in metal and chrome wheelchairs, two on shiny crutches and me with my white cane, all looking cheerful and colourfully dressed, literally stopped the traffic. Indians have a different sense of personal space from us: we often found ourselves at a standstill with people, animals and traffic blocking every visible road while we were gently poked, stroked and patted. Once when I was pushing Eli's wheelchair we found ourselves surrounded with kids, all bending down to peer at Eli's beautiful face as she sat in her bent-forward position. I could see neither her expression nor theirs and said to the back of her head 'Eli, I'd just love to know what expression you have on your face at the moment.' Her reply was 'A beatific smile!'

Our performance in Delhi was to be at the Nehru Centre. When we arrived at midday for a tech run, armed guards were visible on the roof. It had been rumoured that Mrs Ghandi was planning to attend and the sight of the guards certainly lent credence to the rumours. Halfway through our lighting run, we were interrupted by a security guard with a metal detector who marched up on stage and proceeded to wave his clicking, clacking machine in all directions. 'Click' and 'clack' it well might, as there were two wheelchairs, several crutches, my cane and five prop stands on stage, all made of metal. Nigel, usually good natured to the last, yelled at him to get off stage as we were in mid rehearsal and time was short, but this made no impression on the robotically clicking man and machine, who left in his own time without in any way acknowledging the presence of human beings in his metallic world.

Be it the consequence of nerves or years on diuretics for glaucoma, the last thing I do before any performance is go to the loo. I used our travelling portaloo behind a screen backstage, took my place behind the curtain and closed my eyes to begin the centring process I needed before curtain up. Disconcertingly, I realized that the bottoms of my trousers were soaking wet. It then dawned on me that someone must have removed the plastic bag from the portaloo and I had peed all over my trouser bottoms and feet.

I was recovering from this ignominious realization when I heard feet shuffle towards me from the wings. A voice whispered 'The Prime Minister has arrived. Oh, the Prime Minister has arrived. I thought you would all be pleased to know!' And the feet shuffled back into the wings.

The curtain went up and I launched into song, for the first time before a Head of State, peed-on feet and all. After the performance Mrs Ghandi came backstage, dressed very simply in a grey sari. She had a serenity about her and her manner was direct and warm. It was hard to realize that she was also, inevitably, a scheming and ambitious woman. I found myself profoundly shocked when I heard a year later that she had been killed.

On our return to Britain, we were asked to do a three-week tour. Nabs had other commitments and his place was taken by a young Scotsman, Hamish. Hamish and Eli, alas, have both died recently.

My friendship with the complex and contradictory Jag has deepened over the years and I wrote one of my favourite songs for him. It is called 'I Only Believe In Miracles'.

> You are the colour of the sun soaked earth
> With morning still in your eye.
> I am a daughter of the darkening West
> With the sun at noon in my sky.
> So who would ever have believed it?
> Did the water turn to wine?
> Now I only believe in miracles –
> See the rich grape grow on the withered vine.
>
> Your hair is as black as a new moon night,
> Mine streaked like the silvered dawn.
> I had been given the woman's wound
> Before you were ever born.
> So who would ever have believed it?
> Did the man born lame then walk?
> Now I only believe in miracles –
> See the sunflower burst on the shrivelled stalk.
>
> You are a child of the city streets,
> I was raised where wild grasses grew.
> This land has always seemed like home to me,

But to you it was fearful and new.
So who would ever have believed it?
Did the woman who was blind then see?
Now I only believe in miracles –
See the blossom flower on the crippled tree.

You turned from the temple of your birth
To embrace the 'Prince of Peace'
While I lean to the honouring of Mother Earth
And the wisdom from the East.
So who would ever have believed it?
Did the man thought dead then rise?
Now I only believe in miracles
In a fragile flower or a fond friend's eyes.

It was partly this friendship with Jag and heartwarming requests from others that drew me into further involvement with Graeae, which turned out to be a mistake. Graeae had approached the writer/actor Jack Klaff to direct their next show, for the Edinburgh Fringe. I was excited at the prospect of working with Jack and agreed to stay on, keeping several months free for rehearsal and performance. Then, during a preparatory meeting with Jack, the phone rang with news that the Arts Council was not prepared to fund the project. Instead, it was decided to put on a cabaret, produced on a shoestring budget and directed by the company's newly appointed artistic director. I was not keen to be part of this as I couldn't identify with this woman's theatrical approach, but members of the company pleaded with me to stay involved. I also confess that a major reason for staying was the weeks of blank emptiness in my diary: I had not experienced this in years and it scared me somewhat.

I and everyone else learnt the hard way that I should never take on work for the wrong reasons. Day by day I became uneasier about both the quality of performance and the lack of substance in many of the sequences. I was spending an inordinate amount of time pretending, together with another blind actress, that we could see, attempting to waltz between chairs and tables and feeling like a performing horse. I found some scenes tasteless and offensive and knew that anyone with the slightest involvement in the Women's Movement would, too. It dawned on me that for the first time in my life I might be about to find myself at the receiving end of a patronizing audience response along the lines of 'It was really quite good considering that they are disabled.' Since most people who saw me sing didn't even know that I had a visual impairment, the prospect of having an audience 'make allowances' for me in this way was inconceivable. I realized that I couldn't go on without feeling that as an artist, as a woman and as someone with a disability, I was compromising myself.

On the Monday evening of the final rehearsal week, I went to hear the Westbrooks at St James's, Piccadilly. I had sung with Mike and Kate Westbrook, intermittently, for some years, and to me they are truly great artists. Though classified as jazz, their music ranges over a myriad of styles: at the same time, it is always recognizably Westbrook. To my great honour, Mike once did a setting for me of Blake's 'Holy Thursday': their Blake settings, *Bright As Fire*, remain among my most-loved music.

That evening they were performing the Blake suite. Sitting in the glorious Wren church, listening to the sounds of the Brass Band and the sensibilities of William Blake, I knew that I had no choice but to pull out of the cabaret 'For everything that lives is holy'. This wasn't a wimpish sentiment: it was a savage belief in creation and creativity.

After talking with beloved Kate Westbrook I went home and wrote about my feelings and the reasons for them. I made enough copies to give to everyone in the cast and on the staff of Graeae. That Tuesday was one of the most uncomfortable days of my life. I managed to remain clear and assertive: I simply said that on both artistic and ethical grounds I wasn't willing to stay involved.

'But Frankie, what about your professionalism? The show must go on. You can't let us down!'

I could see their point, particularly as many of them were

also unhappy about the piece. The truth was that for many young, disabled, aspiring actors Graeae was the only hope: they needed the company and I didn't. I left sadly, but with tremendous relief. I am now more careful about my motives and more rigorous in choosing who I work with. I still feel sorry to have let down friends and colleagues on this one occasion when I didn't think hard enough before committing myself.

Chapter 17

Some time before my trip to India I reached a strange and disorientating place in my explorations with Buntie. I felt as if I were falling into a deep, dark pit inside me. Though on the surface I went on functioning adequately, the eyes that turned inward saw nothing but death and destruction.

Each age has its topical image for the engulfing darkness; for me, it was the possibility of nuclear strikes by deliberation or accident. The year must have been 1983, Reagan was talking of the 'Antichrist' and the cold war seemed to be intensifying, threatening the entire globe. Believing and fearing that he was mad enough to fight 'the good fight' and destroy us all, I remember feeling towards Reagan something that I can only liken to the murderous rage a mother must feel when invading troops threaten her child. Every nerve felt raw. I saw every child or animal as a helpless victim of this impending devastation. In retrospect I realize that if I had lived at another time, some other set of fears and images would have beset me during this fearful time.

Then, gradually, the intensity of the nightmare subsided. Despair gave way to a deep and abiding sorrow, below the surface most of the time, but there all the same: a sorrow for the Earth and the creatures that inhabit it (including Ronald Reagan!). I have come to recognize how we are all interconnected, which means that we have to find compassion as well as rage, sorrow as well as fury. It also means that I no longer feel split within myself, the way I did when I was also splitting the human race into those worthy only of compassion and those deserving only of anger.

Strangely, it was not a human being that brought me to the most painful point in this sad, sad time, but a black and white stray cat. Zoozie had found her way into our flat at 8 Abbeville Road and into our affections. She had a serenity and grace that enchanted us. She was also an example to me. Buntie once said 'You need to find time to be still. Just think what music would be like if there were never any pauses!' It was when Zoozie curled up on my lap that I found myself simply sitting, for the first time in years in my own home, doing nothing – well, almost nothing. I was actually giving us both intense pleasure by rhythmically stroking her soft fur. When Brian and I came home, we would rattle our keys and this little, miaowing, black and white body would shoot round the side of the house and follow us up to our flat.

I returned from a tiring trip to Glasgow late in October 1983 and Brian met me with the news that Zoozie had been run over. An upstairs neighbour had seen her crawling, injured, into the garden and Brian had spent hours searching for her in the cold and rain, but to no avail. I was devastated: to me she symbolized everything that was innocent and fragile and beautiful, now fallen victim to the inexorable machines that increasingly ruled our lives.

I was due to sing the next day at a Women For Life On Earth conference, but when I woke up in the morning I knew I wasn't capable of singing a note. It's the only time I have ever cancelled a singing engagement as a result of feeling emotionally fragile. While Brian went on searching the gardens around, I wept and wept. In the end we discovered that she had been found and buried by the young man at the little garage across the road, as the police were unable to discover who owned her. He was a lovely young man and talked so gently about burying her in the forecourt of the garage. Hearing this started a healing process that still goes on. The following day we returned with a beautiful rose bush and planted it over her grave.

She was only a little stray cat, but losing her at that time felt like the end of the world to me. At the same time, losing her forced me to take my first step in the crucial process of letting go – the central lesson I had to learn and, indeed, am still learning.

In the weeks that followed, I found a profound solace in an unexpected source. Brian and I were writing the 'song cycle' based around themes, characters and images from the ballad 'Tam Lin'. Brian gave me the words of a song he had written to see if I could find a tune for them. As the melody took shape and the words slowly sank in, I could sense something new happening inside me. It is never easy to describe inner states and even less easy to describe the processes by which we arrive at them. All I can do is to let you see Brian's words, asking you to bear in mind that a song, by definition, does not exist on the page. Sounds and cadences of melody transform the written word. (This is, of course, true of all the songs I have brought into this book, though I have tried to choose those that work to some degree as poetry.)

> Earth, air, fire and water,
> Streams run swift and lakes lie deep.
> The Queen's son weds the old King's daughter.
> In hidden pools the salmon leap.
>
> Earth, water, air and fire,
> The longest night foretells the dawn.
> As day dims the sparks fly higher.
> Brightness bursts from the bitter thorn.
>
> Fire, water, earth and air,
> Round the echoing world the loud winds cry.
> When you reach the end the beginning's there.
> The sun and moon meet in the sky.
>
> Air, water, fire and earth,
> Hope mocks time for evermore
> And every death's a gate to birth.
> Frost splits the rocks but the hills endure.

The words speak better than I can of the change I experienced. To meet the deep, abiding sorrow came a deep, abiding hope and they both live on in me, side by side.

Chapter 18

Demand for my voice workshops was rising steadily, almost entirely through personal contact and word of mouth. I was getting an increasing number of invitations from abroad which, being an enthusiastic traveller, I always did my best to follow up. I learnt to arrange my travels so that I would often do a concert as well as at least one workshop in the same place, moving on from there to a tour which would take me around the country. This way I combined the necessity of earning a living with my enthusiasm for seeing the world and meeting new people.

In 1985 I had my first invitation to Australia. Lindsey Pollack, a young Australian musician who had been to some of my workshops when he was staying in London, proposed to set up concerts and workshops for me there and I accepted eagerly.

It may have been partly because I had no special expectations of Australia that I loved the place immediately. I left a chilly, March London to be met at 3 am by Lindsey and the balmy, scented air of Perth, which had me shedding my London layers down to the T-shirt I had put on in readiness for landing.

When I emerged from a deeply needed sleep I was fed and whisked straight off to the beach: the bright, clean air, the heat, the pounding surf and the glorious galahs, squawking and flitting over our heads, convinced me I had landed in paradise. That Australia isn't paradise becomes clear after a certain time, but I've often been able to recapture something of the magic I experienced on that first day. Not surprisingly I fell for Lindsey. We had a brief romance, but there was no knowing what the future would bring.

I crossed the country to spend four days in Sydney. As I left Perth I knew I was going to miss Lindsey, but I also knew that I wasn't feeling in any way diminished by the separation. I remember feeling happy and thinking 'At last – I feel enough my own woman to take the strength from a relationship along with me, rather than feeling I've left something behind.'

I made a number of lasting friendships in Sydney and discovered an extraordinary quantity of musical talent. It may be because Australian cities are for the most part so isolated that there is more interchange and less competition between artists and less of a concern to fit a mould. Whatever the reasons, I have met composers and musicians of rare talent who are also dedicated to helping others to find their musical creativity.

On my return to England, my newfound strength was tested when Brian told me he had decided to leave. According to our old agreement not to be monogamous, Brian had been seeing Ronno, a social worker from CDP, for some time: we had come to the amicable arrangement that he spent Christmas with me and New Year with her. Now his relationship with Ronno had become very strong. Part of me was prepared, but another part was devastated. I fluctuated between a euphoric independence and a feeling of bewildered disbelief and lostness. We had lived together for 17 years. I always knew that I would survive the adjustment, but there were times when I would find myself feeling very wobbly and disorientated.

But once Brian had made the move, we found a way of being with each other which had all the good things of our companionship and none of the stresses we had sometimes experienced when we lived together.

In June I was off to Canada to sing. Buntie had seen me through my traumas with Brian and I said my fond goodbyes to her, as I always did before the summer break. 'I'll look forward to seeing you in September,' we told each other, as we had done for eight years.

A few weeks later, in Vancouver airport, amid the clatter of teacups and tannoy announcements, I wrote my 'inner engagement' song. Buntie had asked me how the 'inner marriage' was going. 'At least,' I had replied, 'we might be getting engaged.' The song was called 'Meeting':

He came down from the mountain, bearing the sun like a halo,
She came up from the valley, casting a long black shadow.
Will their steps cross, will their paths meet,
and what will they say when they greet?

He came in from the desert where the land lay parched and fallow.
She came up from the darkness, from the depth of a water hollow.
Will their paths merge, will their steps meet,
and what will they feel when they greet?

He strode through the tall pines on a path cut straight as an arrow.
She strolled by a wandering stream hidden by briars and willow.
Will their hands touch, will their eyes meet,
and what will they do when they greet?

He climbed down a steep cliff where the ledges were dangerous and narrow.
She swam up through a turquoise sea to where waters lay still and shallow.
Will their ways meet there on the shore
and will they both know what it's for?

I was never to see Buntie again. I heard that she was ill, though there was still hope that she might be well enough to start 'term' again in September. I was due to return to Australia in mid-October. When there was still no word from her by early October, I realized that her illness was serious and it came to me that she might be dying. Strangely enough, it was not a terrible shock. It was rather as if I already knew. All that inner work on 'surrender' seemed to be a preparation for Brian's leaving and for losing Buntie.

Shortly before I left on that second visit to Australia, I had a phone call from Eric Maddern, my good friend Rosemary's ex-housemate from Adelaide. He wanted a tape of my song 'Message for Mother Earth', to use in a theatre project on evolution and ecology that he was setting up in London. He mentioned in passing that he was looking for somewhere to stay.

I needed someone to stay in the flat and look after the cats while I went to Australia, so, on the day I left for Australia, Eric moved in. I handed him the keys and he handed me two cassettes of songs he had written and recorded, one for Rosemary and the other for another friend, Darien.

Rosemary was back in Adelaide by then and we stayed together in a beautiful converted barn for the first of the workshops she had arranged. On the Sunday morning I awoke from a vivid dream. I was sitting on the edge of Buntie's bed. She was curled up in a foetal position, very small and shrunken and so light I could cradle her in my arms like a baby. Her face was still soft and beautiful. I said goodbye and the dream faded.

It wasn't until Thursday morning that Lois managed to reach me by phone and tell me that Buntie had died on the previous Monday.

I had said goodbye to her early that Sunday morning, the day before she died. The Thursday I heard about her death was the day of my concert. I spent the morning weeping. In the afternoon I visited Cleland Wildlife Park with a group of Rosemary's friends. There was great comfort in patting kangaroos and listening to the haunting songs of the native birds. Before the concert Darien, who ran a professional massage school, and whom I had met for the first time that same morning, gave me a neck and shoulder massage which helped to relax and centre me. It was one of the best concerts I have ever given and I managed to keep from crying on stage. Even with the saddest song or occasion, it is my belief that while my artistry may have the audience weep, my craft must keep me from doing so. I told the audience that I had heard earlier that day of the death of an older woman who had been central in my life: telling them seemed to make it possible to channel my feelings through the songs.

I have felt your presence so close, so often, dearest Buntie, and I have also been able to let you go. I was one of the lucky ones. You helped to prepare me for loss – for the loss of Brian, for the possible loss of my sight and ultimately for the loss of you. You are so in evidence in whatever is best in my personal and working life that I will be for ever grateful for the time we had together. You were an immensely wise friend, teacher of the soul and spirit – a guide towards wholeness and a funny, eccentric woman. You did what you aimed to do: you helped me to become more truly myself.

Darien

Chapter 19

It was only hours after my farewell dream about Buntie that Sunday morning in Adelaide that Darien walked into my workshop. He was noticeable as a latecomer, his car having broken down on the way. I remember how impressed I was with his hands. They were long-fingered, strong and very gentle.

'I've been told you don't see much. Would you like to feel my face to get a sense of me?' This could have seemed egotistical, but from the tone of his voice and manner it was clear to me that this was not so: he was simply interested in the sense of touch and intrigued as to how I 'saw' the world. It was he who had taken my hand on the day I had heard of Buntie's death and laid it gently on the back of a browsing kangaroo.

Next day he phoned to tell me that the concert was the most moving and intelligent he had ever been to. I was of course flattered; I was also intrigued to find out what criteria led him to feel this way. He talked of his approach to the tactile senses and to movement in similar terms to those I use about sound and song (the movement of vocal sounds). It was one of those stimulating, confirming conversations that leave you eager for more.

I started dropping strong hints in his direction over the next days, but he seemed fairly impervious. The day before I was due to return to Perth, he invited me for a stroll along the beach at Glenelg. He was handing me shells, pebbles and seaweed to feel. I thought 'Well, here goes!' I told him I found him very attractive and would like a chance to spend more time with him, adding hopefully 'You don't have any plans to visit Sydney in January, do you?'

As a matter of fact he did, though he wasn't sure just which part of the month he'd be there. I told him I would be flying back to Britain on the 21st. We hugged goodbye and he said it was possible that we might meet up in Sydney.

Two days later I was in the south of Western Australia and Darien was still somewhere on my mind. Was I in love? No, this didn't seem to fit – not yet, anyway. What in heaven's name was I feeling? I was in the shower when the response to this query bubbled up in the form of a song. I called it 'Invitation'.

Well I'm not in love, and I'm not in lust,
But it's more than infatuation
and there's something here that I'm sure I should trust –
Maybe I'm in anticipation.

I can sleep at night, and I'm eating fine,
Though this could be compensation
and there's tingles still run up and down my spine –
Maybe I'm in strong inclination.

I'm not singing songs of moon and June,
Though writing this could have implications
and it's such a delight to sing a new tune –
Maybe I'm in inspiration.

There is no rush. Let the tale unfold.
I'm not dying of frustation,
but I still feel your touch from the day I was bold –
Maybe I'm in heightened sensation.

Then came Christmas. I was to spend the evening of Christmas Eve and all of Christmas day with friends: the first Christmas I'd ever spent without either my parents or Brian. I had no idea how I would feel. To my delight, I woke up feeling calm and cheerful. I decided to ring Brian and Ronno in London and Rosemary in Adelaide. All the lines to Britain were busy, so I spoke to Rosemary first.

She said 'Have you heard from Darien yet?' I said I had not. 'Well, you will! The day you left he was round at my house asking endless questions about you. He's definitely going to Sydney while you're there.'

That felt like a pretty good Christmas present. Then I got a free line to London and had an enjoyable chat with Brian and Ronno, which somehow felt like a good omen. During the year, I had to let go of Brian, then Lindsey, then Buntie. Sad as these losses had made me, I had also found a strength in letting go. I felt calmer than I could remember.

Darien did come to Sydney. He stayed with Bruce Russell, a social worker and writer he had met at the First National Men's Festival. I enjoyed being with the two of them: their conversation struck me as more akin to the kind of conversations women have than the usual fare that passes for intimacy between men. I had to look at my reactions when Darien said he couldn't see me because he wanted to spend the evening with Bruce. Then I realized that my initial, hurt reaction was ridiculous, as I had always made time to see my women friends and regarded that as a priority in my life.

By the end of two weeks together I knew I was in love. I had a disturbing dream in which I was trying to reach Darien by phone and the dial seemed to melt and I couldn't get through. I found myself being pierced by arrows which didn't wound me; they were telling me something had hit my heart. I woke up feeling distraught. At the same time, I was even more certain that 'there is something here I'm sure I should trust.'

I had to get on that plane back to England on January 21st. How soon could I return? With a little juggling of engagements, I found I could be back in Australia around early May. Over the four months before my return to Adelaide, enough cassette tape passed between Darien and me to encircle the planet. Our collective phone bills would have paid for at least one return fare to Australia. It was a good time.

I did manage to concentrate on some other things while I was in England, including creating an enormously stimulating performance with the very talented singer and theatre director, Joan Mills. We took as our theme women being trapped – behind prison walls and social conventions, as witches and suffragettes, for refusing to marry men their fathers chose for them, being raped by gaolers, fathers, brothers or strangers. We wept with these women, screamed with them, implored and prayed with them. Through improvisation, text and song we raged, found pride and defiance and an inner strength that was, in itself, a release. Images and situations gradually emerged to form our play, which we called *Lost Voices*.

There were only three performances and not a second was wasted in their creation. Working consistently on such potent material brought us into an empathy that transferred itself into our voices. It has stayed with us ever since. Heard separately, there is no doubt whose voice is whose: Joan's voice has an unmistakable, bell-like resonance. When this is combined with my somewhat darker and edgier quality, it's as if we make a third voice out of the two. When we can find that balance between us, something very magical can happen.

I organized enough work in Adelaide, Melbourne and Sydney to finance my return to Australia and went back in May.

I had a glorious week with Darien in the southern Flinders Ranges, under the shadow of Mount Remarkable, staying in a little cottage which had basic electricity but no running water. At night it was freezing cold, so we gathered wood and sat huddled in front of a log fire. I collected the water and wood and made up the fire while Darien did the cooking.

On our daily walks into the mountains I grew to love the birdsong, to recognize some of the main trees by their leaves and smells and, through my misty vision, to get a feel for the colours of rocks and vegetation: it's only this year that I've been able to revel in the astonishing scenery of southern Australia.

When Darien went to California for the third leg of his Feldenkreis training I went with him. And there we began to put together joint workshops we called 'Full Bodied Voice Workshops'. Our approach and skills turned out to be complementary and since then we have adapted a wide range of relaxation and physical awareness exercises. We went on travelling together, back to Australia for a short trip up to Alice Springs and on to the tropical north coast of Darwin.

By the time we reached Darwin it was clear that Darien and I were going to spend considerable chunks of each year living and working together. It was also becoming clear that things would be much easier if we were married: for one thing, we wouldn't have to hassle constantly with work permits. I was by now 45 and Darien 38. I had many objections to marriage as an institution, but found these more easily overruled than I would have thought. So, we took the plunge and hoped. Once it was decided, I discovered a certain romantic enjoyment of the prospect. I phoned Mum and casually dropped 'This afternoon I went shopping for a dress to get married in.' My parents hadn't met Darien, but they had heard him on tape and seen photos. Mum sounded delighted and Dad said warmly 'Tell him from me he's an exceptionally lucky man.'

Ten days before the wedding I had an affirming dream: I went into a travel agency, said that I was going on a journey and asked to look at their brochures. As I left, the charming man behind the counter asked if he could take me out. I thanked him warmly, but declined, saying, 'I may not be sure where I'm going, but I know who I'm going with!'

In Australia it's possible to marry outside a church or registry office, so we decided to hold the wedding in Cleland, the wildlife park where the kangaroo patting had taken place. We were told we could hold the ceremony at 5 pm, after the public had left, if we made a small financial gift to the park.

When December 21st arrived, a cool wind was blowing in from the southern Antarctic. I wore a cotton sun dress, covered with flowers and fruit in vibrant colours, with a shawl to protect me against goose bumps. I avoided the goose bumps, but not the geese!

We chose a spot by the lake with a range of water birds, including pied geese. We had created our own 'service' – which was not conventionally religious, and included poems, other writings and songs, which a friend was tape-recording. Tai, aged 12, was the official photographer.

The tape is hilarious. As the readings began, they were accompanied by the incessant honking of the geese, which came closer and closer until they were clambering in our baskets, tugging at our hems and nibbling at our toes. By this time we could hardly make ourselves heard.

Darien's voice comes over, half annoyed, half amused, 'I think I'd like to move!'

In the end we spoke our vows and sang our songs higher up the hill, surrounded by kangaroos. They browsed contentedly, taking no notice of the small circle of people talking and weeping and laughing, until Darien began playing his guitar to accompany a song he had written for me. At this they stood up on their hind legs, tilted their heads to one side and looked at him curiously with those large, dark eyes. Tai captured them beautifully in his snapshots.

A few weeks later, when we were working in Sydney, our wedding was celebrated all over again. Our dear musician-singer friends, Moya Stokes and John Shortis, threw a nuptial party with an amazing musical line-up including Margaret Roadknight, Judy Small and Mara and Llew Keik. John and Moya wrote and previewed a hilarious song that night, presenting us with a framed copy of the words, which accurately describes how we had spent our first night together in their house exactly a year before: how the slatted bed had collapsed under us and the Alsatian had howled his head off in response to our hilarity.

We might have got married, but we saw no reason to do what everyone expected us to do and 'settle down'. However, it did become clear that it made little sense to keep a home on each side of the globe. We needed to base ourselves on one continent or the other, and eventually we decided to make Britain our base, with annual visits to Australia.

We have a much wider range of work opportunities within travelling distance in Europe – if we had lived in Australia we would have been longer on the road, and would have seen each other less often. But I don't underestimate the sacrifice Darien has made in leaving his intimate circle of friends.

We settled eventually in Cardiff, within reach of real countryside and mountains, and near to John Mills, with whom I hoped to work further.

A few days ago we were walking in the Caerphilly Hills. The sheep and lambs glowed white against the green hills and distant dogs barked from the white farm houses dotted over the landscape. I followed Darien up to the edge of the pine trees, a mass of bluebells in their shelter. We enjoy one another as companions, lovers and working colleagues, and I have every hope that this will continue. Darien is a rare man, with qualities and values I can respect.

Vision

Chapter 20

So my story begins to catch up with my life, the past merging into the present. I had known for some years that a cataract operation could eventually be performed which might restore a significant amount of sight to my eye, but there was also a serious risk that it might take away what little sight I still had. My feeling was that I could only undertake this operation when I could totally accept this idea that what had happened to my sight in the past had been my fate – something I had needed in order to learn what I had to learn.

Looking back over my life, all that I had been lucky enough to experience and learn, I came to realize this was indeed what I would have chosen for myself. This gave me the confidence I needed to book my bed at Moorfields, as I now felt I could accept the outcome of the operation, whatever it might be. I felt that the spring of 1990 would be the right time and I was offered a date in early June. This was when I decided to write my life story and I wrote the opening lines in the form of a diary. That entry began this book and as I look at the diary now, I see it is the best way, to tell of my life from there.

6 June 1990, Moorfields Hospital
The past 24 hours have surely been a test of how deep is my understanding of William Blake's wise observation that we see through, not with, our eyes. It is some years since I first heard this on the radio. As I reflected on it then, a new understanding dawned that was to change my attitude to my then failing sight. I recognized that the physical act of seeing was not the important one. For this reason, whatever happens to my eye, it doesn't really matter.

Yesterday, coming round from the anaesthetic in the

recovery room, I was amazed at how calm I felt and, in a strange way, how incurious. It is a great release to realize that, even at the moment of not knowing, I could accept whatever I was to find.

Within hours it was evident that I could still see light. I had been expecting to wake up with a pad or bandages over my eye. There was nothing of the sort: just a plastic shield with little holes in it, through which light was clearly visible. I took a childish delight in switching my bedside lamp on and off, to reassure myself that I could tell the difference. As I have virtually no sight in the eye they were not operating on, this perception of light had to be through the right eye.

An hour after my return from the theatre the houseman lifted the shield off my eye and I was startled by the almost translucent brightness flooding in. I realized then that I could see, but I had no idea how much. The shield was off for a matter of minutes while drops were put in and, though I could see something, it was all swimming about in post-operative watering and inflammation. I was excited, but had to wait until this morning to know more.

I woke early with the memory of a dream in which I was delightedly showing my father what I could see, pointing out colours to him, just as later on this very day I was to do in reality with my mother.

The Consultant, John Wright, shone bright lights in my eye and said 'This seems to be looking good.' He sounded pleased, saying what a technically tricky operation it had been, though we both know that it is too early to start talking about success: serious complications can so easily intervene in the hours immediately after such an operation.

The plastic shield that was over my eye yesterday has been removed and here I am in this world of moving Modigliani paintings. Contrasting lines and shapes emerge and retreat. Colours more vivid than I ever recall in a King's College Chapel window swim into focus. My bedside table and tray are festooned with flowers brought by beloved friends: I can scarcely believe the brilliant blue of the cornflowers, the rich redness of carnations and roses. Roses and roses and more roses, delicate pinks, deep flame orange, white and red. It is literally a case of not being able to believe my eye.

Strangest of all is being able to see Darien, for the first time. He has been joking that maybe I will want to divorce him once I can see him. To my surprise, he didn't look as I had expected. Of course, I know his features intimately by touch and I had created my own pictures. But on seeing him, he is more craggy – I suppose more 'masculine' – than the image I had conjured. I find the expressivity of his face intriguing: how features come together in motion is fascinating and this is something you can never get by feel. It will take us both some time to adjust to seeing and being seen.

I have seen other friends I made more recently, as well as Mum and friends I can remember seeing. What has surprised me is how little they have changed. Perhaps it helps that I can't see the minutiae of our lines and wrinkles!

It is now evening at the close of one of life's more blessed days. I have been given some glasses with thick, somewhat magnifying lenses, with which I can see more clearly than I have for at least 15 years. I have seen visiting friends and family as one would in a painting by Sisley or Monet – painters I loved in my teens and twenties when I was still able to enjoy paintings with the aid of a monocular.

Today's experiences have been like reopening the door into the world of the visual artist. On the wall just outside the ward is a reproduction of Corot's view of a serene autumn scene, the filigree arms of bare trees spreading into a white sky, the simple buildings across the river reflected in still water and two small figures perfectly placed in the landscape. I feel profound joy at all that has been revealed to me in the course of this one day. But even deeper is my feeling of peace at the knowledge that, sad as I would have been had the outcome been different, I would still have been able to see 'through' my eyes.

7 June

I doubt that the view from the hospital's first floor window overlooking City Road really bears much resemblance to a

Utrillo painting, yet at 7 am, as the sun slid its way through the vertical gaps, it was Utrillo that came to mind. I found myself struggling to make sense of horizontal and vertical lines as I looked at the world with unaccustomed eye: roofs intersecting the early morning skyline, tiers of windows punctuating the pale grey frontages and, unlike Utrillo, silent cars slipping in and out of the junction below. It is like a dream – indeed, for more than a decade it has only been in dreams that I have seen such things.

12 June

In the days that followed the operation it was difficult to bear the constant stimulus and sheer brightness of the new/old world around me, so I spent part of each day wearing plain tinted glasses to rest from it all.

Today, when Mum, Darien and I stepped out of Moorfields Hospital into the gentle rain at around 7.30 pm, the June evening was more akin to April, sun and showers mixing themselves confusedly through the afternoon. In spite of the rain there was a decided glow from the west. The cars had their headlights on. To me the lights reflecting off the tarmac road and the colours glistening with the rain looked like a fairyland. This is somewhat ironical, as I also think cars are an abomination which, for the health of the planet and its inhabitants, should be severely culled. I was able to enjoy a more wholehearted delight in the bright red buses which give me less ideological wobble.

By this time we were driving through the traffic and I had put on my thick-lensed glasses to find colour and definition, the likes of which I can barely remember – though I must have enjoyed this quality of sight around 20 years ago. Strangely, I now realize that I carried a much stronger visual memory for paintings, films, dreams and the creations of the imagination than for everyday surroundings in a city. I had forgotten how many trees there were in Central London.

On entering my friend's flat in Kew where we are to stay for the next week or so, I found it quite changed. I have visited Lois in her home many times before, but now I could see paintings and hangings on the walls, large plants in the front window and again, everywhere, colour.

I had left hospital with enough flowers to set up a florist's business. While Mum found vases and containers to display them on every available surface, Darien and I strolled over the road towards the Thames towpath. Going down Ship Alley in the direction of the river, we heard a greeting 'Miaow!' The timing was perfect. As we approached, an exquisite black and white cat leaned over the wall above our heads and, in the glowing dusk, I could see her fine whiskers and pointed ears silhouetted above. She purred and rubbed and miaowed and we danced our duet of delight.

I will never forget our few hundred yards' stroll that evening. The lights shining from across the river were reflecting in the water. The willow patterned itself against mud. Water and sky, white, purple and pink flowers, all leapt out to greet us. Lights came on in the houses and pubs and the ornamental gas lamps sprang alight along the towpath. This portion of Strand-on-the-Green has to be one of the loveliest parts of London.

My new glasses make my eyes look twice their normal size. In these days of exploration as I visit shops, pubs, gardens, Darien insists that these big eyes are well suited to the four-year-old who is endlessly pointing out newly discovered colours and objects.

21 June
Some memories from the first days after my operation still make me laugh.

Seeing people's legs again has, for some reason, been hilariously funny: perhaps it is partly my eye watering, making legs, particularly legs in trousers, wobble about in an unsteady manner at the bottom of people's bodies. I have seen trousered legs in many a dream over the past dimly-sighted years, so why I can't stop laughing at their appearance now, remains a mystery.

The day after the operation, I lay in the bath and suddenly thought 'Whose body is this in the bath with me?' It took me some time to 'own' these feet with toes visibly wiggling at the end of my legs. Even now, being able to see my feet, often clad in brightly coloured socks and shoes, is a source of great excitement.

I visited my mother's flat, previously experienced only by touch and the vaguest visual impression. When I wandered into the bathroom and saw the coloured towels, my thought was 'It's much better since Mum put in this bright lighting!'

Next day I walked up a favourite hill, Fontmell Down. I found I could discern distances in a way I haven't been able to for a very long time: the closer fields with the brighter, deeper colours, and the distant Blackmoor Vale, of Hardy fame, fading off paler and bluer into the distance.

Driving home to Cardiff, Darien and I were treated to a spectacular light show. The sky had been almost unrelievedly clouded since I left hospital but now, as we drove through Wiltshire, an apricot streak transformed itself into a line of translucent gold, streaming out from under deep blue-purple cloud. By the time we came to the Mendips, the sun was shedding brilliant rays across the hills and setting trees and hillside alight with its radiance. This was probably a very ordinary sunset, but to my unaccustomed eye it was truly spectacular.

Though it has rained steadily since our return to Cardiff, I love this place and the hills and woods around. Last evening we drove out to an area of woods and streams which in the damp dusk looked like something out of Arthur Rackham: so many shapes twisting and turning – roots, branches, leaves, stone-strewn paths, eddying water. It will be interesting to see how long this freshness of vision remains with me.

23 June

Each day brings fresh miracles, yet while I feel the full blessing of seeing more than I ever anticipated, I am aware that this is a bonus and not an essential. There are so many visually handicapped people who live life to the full and are able to discover dimensions that many sighted people miss out on. Had things worked out differently, I would have counted myself among their number still and would not have gone around wishing for the return of more sight. I know that, paradoxically, the failure of my sight was a great gift, one that taught me so many lessons, and I have no doubt that I am a richer person for the experience.

30 June
Just occasionally, now, I catch myself taking this gift for granted – only to be brought up against some new realization: absentmindedly picking a piece of fluff off Darien's jumper and realizing the implications of this only seconds later; seeing the steam rise from my coffee cup or the Alsatian in the next door garden chasing his splendid tail round in circles; seeing rain drops illuminated by the headlights of a car.

Mum has always been able to see 'eternity in a grain of sand', but I have taken a long time to learn this great and simple art. The past three and a half weeks have brought Blake's image clearly and literally to life. All children, unless profoundly damaged, have this sense of wonder as they look at the world, but all too often this vision shrivels under the pressures of adult life. I feel immensely privileged to have been granted this fresh vision again.

May 1991
I have been enjoying my restored vision now for nearly a year. One of the great gains has been the freedom this brings to walk in the country and explore the streets of unfamiliar towns on my own. I have come to recognize a profound change in myself, since I would not in the past have felt that a beautiful landscape was complete unless I was sharing it with another. I now find that I positively enjoy walking un-accompanied through countryside – indeed time on my own is something I have come to need. This freedom is one of the most precious gifts that my consultant's skilled fingers have given me.

I have revisited beloved landscapes, including the Welsh mountains where I first realized that my sight was threatened.

I have also seen for the first time the astonishing shapes and colours of the Australian landscape, of which I had only the haziest impression before this year.

As well as recovering distant vision, I can see well enough to pick out detail with the help of a monocular supplied to me by Moorfields hospital.

One of my greatest delights has been to see Brian and Ronno's first baby, now three months old. Loving Brian so dearly and having learnt to love Ronno, this feels like the closest I shall ever get to the magic of birth. Ieuan has blue, blue almond-shaped eyes like Brian. He looks at us all so knowingly. His favourite thing in the world, after Mum's milk, is being sung to. Ronno was told she couldn't sing, yet there she is, improvising wonderful tunes and funny, surreal rhyming couplets. I wonder if there is any mother who doesn't sing to her newborn? It's such a clear indication of the naturalness of song.

Epilogue

Chapter 21

4 June 1991

It is exactly one year since I began writing my story. As I write these words, I find myself back in my beloved Lake District. Darien and I are staying in Buttermere for a few days and today has been our first opportunity since the operation to go walking on these fells. I have marvelled at the panorama of the mountains, watching the shadows of the clouds scudding across the hillsides and the patches of bright spring green appearing where the sun finds a way through. I find myself surprised by the vivid colour of the golden gorse and delighted by the black and white of the Herdwick sheep and the more pristinely contrasting black and white of the lambs. This morning we watched sheepdogs from the farm where we are staying as they streaked across the fells, herding the ewes and their offspring and driving them up to new pastures.

From the top of Robinson Crag we had a view over Buttermere, Crummock Water and Loweswater and way across to the coast and the Irish Sea. Darien could see quite clearly as far as Workington, the place where I was born, which I wrote about on that first day in hospital one year ago. I can imagine no better way to celebrate this anniversary than enjoying the song of the Lakeland larks and the croakings of the ravens while viewing this most loved of all landscapes.

It has been a rich year writing this book. It has made me more aware of the mystery at the heart of each and every one of our existences. I feel I have been immensely lucky to have been given clear signposts on my particular, peculiar journey. The signposts have led me to people and places that have profoundly influenced my life and thought. I am acutely aware of the blessings that are loved ones, family, friends, many of whom have been mentioned in this book, others left out owing to lack of space.

I am aware of one important thread that has been present throughout but hardly mentioned since the opening chapters. My parents and my brother Tony have remained in the background, always in touch with me and supporting my endeavours: it is the very constancy and blessed sameness of their presence that has kept them in that background, while more changing and turbulent matters have occupied my attention.

Mum and Dad were in Windermere for some years after Dad's retirement, enjoying walks in the hills and playing a lot of golf. Then they wisely decided to move south again while they were still in good health and bought a flat on top of the hill in Shaftesbury, a few miles from the farm that my brother Tony manages with Mary, his wife, and their four sons.

There was a time, a year or two before they moved south, when Dad and I became quite intolerant and irritable with one another. Dad was 6ft 8ins tall and good looking in a craggy way, which led to his being somewhat imposing in manner: people tended not to challenge his actions or criticize him head-on. We knew him to be fundamentally a just man so in the family we would simply grit our teeth and bear with his sometimes arbitrary decisions.

One afternoon he was driving me to Oxenholme station to get a train. Mum was in the back seat. Dad had arranged for Brian's climbing boots to be re-soled and we had thanked him over the telephone, but now, as we drove along, Dad remarked with a note of sarcasm, 'Tell Brian it would be nice to get a word of thanks for the trouble I went to over his boots. A stamp only costs 10p!'

I felt a rising fury: this time I took a deep breath and let fly. 'Dad, that is simply unreasonable. We thanked you over the phone. I'm not willing to be a messenger of what I believe to be pettiness!'

There was a stunned silence. In the 20 minutes it took to get to the station, I could feel Mum getting agitated. Dad pulled up and turned off the engine. He shifted in his seat and leant towards me, putting his silver white head to mine. 'You'll have to forgive your old dad. He gets a bit daft in his old age, from time to time.'

As we sat there, I'm sure we all had tears in our eyes. I hugged and thanked him and got out to catch my train. From that day on, we never found ourselves on our old battle-ground, but would always manage to head off any conflict before it developed.

Dad became softer, even playful, as he grew older. When I took Darien to meet my parents after we got married, he got on well with both of them and we were all surprised when Dad allowed Darien to give him a massage. And, to my further surprise, Darien later made a gift to my father – a cuddly, pale blue hippopotamus from a zoo in the wilds of Australia, which Dad promptly named Henrietta and treasured for the rest of his life. In January 1988, for his birthday, we sent him another bright blue hippo with large saucer eyes from Adelaide – Henrietta's companion Horace.

Three months after that I returned from one trip to Australia, several weeks ahead of Darien. Brian met me with the news of Dad's sudden death four days before. He had died in his sleep without prior warning. Mum and I were left with no unresolved feelings – we had both told him of our love for him so often. Because of the time he had been born into, he had not been able to live his life quite as he would have wanted: he was happiest out of doors and would have been better suited by work in forestry or farming, but oppor-tunities were limited in those fields. He made as good a job of his life as he knew how, adored Mum and worked dutifully to provide for us all.

Mum went through the inevitable shock and numbness and a period of self-reproach, but her simple love of life and people became more evident as time went on.

One day she said to me, 'I think some of the neighbours may be a little shocked at how I've got on with my life, how I'm really enjoying new aspects of it. I think they must feel that I didn't really love Jimmy, but you know I did and always will. I'm just so grateful for a happy marriage of nearly 50 years, grateful for you and Tony and how fulfilled you both are – and grateful that Jimmy went so peacefully and didn't have a long, painful illness.'

I found myself laughing. 'D'you know that many of us have spent thousands of pounds on therapy or following this or that guru or spiritual discipline in hopes of eventually being able to "love and let go"? And you've managed it by being yourself, living simply and honestly!'

'Love and let go,' she reflected. 'Yes, that describes what I feel exactly. Isn't that wonderful? That's a big help, to put a name to it.'

When I think about my family, I still find myself including Brian in it. I am thankful that he and I have remained close friends. Ronno has also become very important to me: one Christmas we bought Brian a pair of expensive climbing boots – a boot from each of us, a good symbol, I think, of our capacity for non-possessively sharing him. And, having once found a generosity within ourselves, we discovered an unshakable trust.

Our annual trips to Australia are partly to keep in touch with Darien's father, Hal, a wonderfully eccentric and interesting man: a retired architect with long white hair and a white beard. He lives in Adelaide and I love visiting him.

Now that we are settled in Cardiff, I begin to find myself in demand for voice workshops and concerts here and in the Welsh valleys, which gives me hope that I may begin to spend more of my year working from home. We have a garden and I find myself becoming more and more involved in the process of planting and watching out for the expected flowers to appear. This is the fulfilment of a lifelong ambition. Darien has also begun to put down roots by organizing courses based in Cardiff. But we are still open to exciting and distant invitations.

As a result of working on this book I now count amongst my fond circle Jenny Pearson, without whom this book could never have been shaped and brought to fruition.

I count myself lucky to be a woman who has a partner who is gentle and considerate, trusting and trustworthy, and can sometimes show this by standing up to me when my tendency to railroad others requires it.

I count myself amongst those privileged people who work at what they love. I enjoy equally the act of singing songs to those wishing to listen; running workshops for those wishing to explore and develop their voices; offering others the opportunity to train with me in my idiosyncratic approach; and the opportunities to work in the world of drama and theatre. I hope I will be able to continue weaving these vivid strands out of the tapestry of voice. As for vision, I feel myself to have been granted two great gifts: one, the gift of losing my sight and the strengths, perceptions and understandings this has brought me; secondly, the gift of having enough sight restored to wonder daily at the marvels nature creates around us. Through vision, as well as my other heightened senses, I feel myself to be constantly surrounded by everyday miracles.

I still feel immense gratitude towards William Blake for the insight contained in the verse I first heard on that radio programme many years ago.

This life's five windows on the soul
Distort the heavens from pole to pole,
And lead you to believe a lie,
When you see with, not thro', the eye.

If indeed we see 'through,' not 'with' our eyes, then with or without the physical capacity to see, we can still be blessed with vision.

Ways of Seeing (written in 1988)

There are many ways I cannot see
In a world of blurring shapes and colour,
But that's no cause to be sad for me,
It makes my vision all the fuller.

It was a wise teacher who broke the ties
When he said 'I see through, not with my eyes.'

I see swirling suns and a mirrored moon
In the night when dreams seem all the clearer,
And landscapes drawn by sound and tune
Make the hearing all the richer.

It was a wise singer who broke the ties
When he said 'I see through, not with my eyes.'

In memory I clearly see
The vibrant rose, the sunflower's yellow,
The laburnum and the lilac tree,
Still waters that reflect the willow.

It was a wise artist who broke the ties
When he said 'I see through, not with my eyes.'

In my mind's eye are gliding birds,
Fish that dart through the turquoise water,
Pictures conjured by the spell of words,
The ballad and the storyteller.

It was a wise poet who broke the ties
When he said 'I see through, not with my eyes.'

There is vision not sensed by sight
An insight born of loss and grieving,
To face the darkness, face the night,
Brings lightness and a heart's rejoicing.

It was a wise seer who broke the ties
When he said 'I see through, not with my eyes.'